Pat McKinzie-Lechault

HOME SWEET HARDWOOD

A TITLE IX TRAILBLAZER BREAKS BARRIERS THROUGH BASKETBALL

PAT MCKINZIE-LECHAULT

FOREWORD BY JILL HUTCHISON

Home Sweet Hardwood
A Title IX Trailblazer Breaks Cultural Barriers Through Basketball

Website: http://pattymackz.com/wordpress/book/

Some of the names have been changed.

First printing – fourth edition June 2013
ISBN: 1477465979
ISBN-13: 978-1477465974
Library of Congress Control Number: 2012920399
North Charleston, SC

Manufactured in the United States of America

Advance Praise

"*Home Sweet Hardwood*" is both a gut-wrenching and uplifting journey through the growing pains of women's sports, written by one of its most determined pioneers."

Jackie "Mac" McMullen
NBA columnist for ESPN
Geno: In Pursuit of Perfection with Geno Auriemma and Diana Taurasi 2006
Shaq Uncut My Story with Shaquille O'Neal 2011

"Pat McKinzie-Lechault is a living legacy — the granddaughter of a legendary coach, Eureka College's Ralph McKinzie, and the protégé of one of women's basketball's pioneers, Illinois State's Jill Hutchison. Her writing style brings the picture to the reader as she 'pays forward' her gratitude for an amazing life where, truly, her home was the hardwood."

Tom Lamonica
Sports information director, Illinois State University (1980-2006)

"Pat was truly a pioneer paving the way for numerous young girls wanting to have an opportunity to excel in sports. She set the bar high when she was competing and now Pat maintains the same high standards by educating, coaching and mentoring students every day. I was privileged to work with her daughter, Nathalie, for four years at UWSP. Thank you Pat for all you have done for the game we both love."

Shirley Egner
Women's Basketball Coach University of Wisconsin-Stevens Point
NCAA Champion 2001-02, Final Four 2003-04

"*Home Sweet Hardwood* is a story about "what if's." Pat McKinzie-Lechault is an example of a woman who took advantage of a "what if" and became a trailblazer. One wonders what our world would be like if women had taken advantage of their desires to participate in sport, like men, without feeling wrong to do so. I am convinced that if we had more women like Pat, our world would have more balanced leadership and positive role models."

Cary Groth
Athletic Director University of Nevada since 2005
Athletic Director Northern Illinois University 1994-2004

"Thank you Pat for being one of my silent heroes! I am proud to say that I followed in your shoes and earned an athletic scholarship to I.S.U. In my life and career as a professional basketball player, I am an *adventuras* person living abroad and teaching what I've learned from you, my family, Coach Hutchison and Coach Fischer to young basketball players."

Cathy Boswell
1984 Olympic Gold Medalist Women's Basketball
Coach at Tenerife, Canary Islands

"Pat McKinzie was a phenomenal athlete, but, most importantly, an exceptional human being and teammate. Her story proves that if you have a dream, believe in it, visualize it, and are passionate about it, you will achieve it, so never give up! Women of our generation faced obstacles as athletes. Title IX gave us a break, but it was no guarantee. We reached our goals the old fashioned way – through persistence, hard work and conviction. In doing so, we paved the way for future generations of female athletes. Women like Pat set an example for today's athletes to follow their dream with passion and determination. We did – and look where it got us!"

Cindy L. Bower, *CHA*
Founder & CEO, Calibre Management, Inc.
Owner and Operator of Nature-based Resorts

"This poignant story is a powerful reminder to the young women and girls of today that the right to equal opportunities was a hard fought battle. It also speaks volumes to those increasing numbers of families who are facing cross-cultural challenges of their own as they relocate for work, love, or service in this ever globalizing world."

Tina Quick
CEO, International Family Transitions
2011 Gold Medalist Basketball Senior Games

"I've heard it said that "each of us is more than the work we've ever done" and yet, as advocates, we continue to do the work we're called to do. In childhood, Pat McKinzie's passion for the game of basketball surfaced. It wasn't until an equal rights bill was passed in 1972 that she was able to participate in the sport, following in the footsteps of her father and grandfather. An accident at the height of her career caused a devastating setback. Ever the champion, she survived and reconstructed her life. A writer, teacher and coach, Pat continues to mentor and make a difference in the lives of women and girls.

Home Sweet Hardwood is a memoir on life...love... and the struggles and triumphs of being a basketball globetrotter and what it meant for girls who wanted to play the game during a time when it was considered "taboo."

A women's advocate, I find myself inspired by the sheer endurance and determination this woman has maintained on her journey from recovery to empowerment. Even if you've never been privy to the game of women's basketball, reading this book will cause you to come away with a brand new respect for the game and for the women who dared to step up and step into a sport once meant for the "boys."

With *Home Sweet Hardwood*, Pat McKinzie again steps to the challenge, faces the goal and makes a slam dunk!"

Clara Freeman
Author and women's advocate
CEO Authentic Woman Networks

Pat McKinzie-Lechault

Table of Contents

Home Sweet Hardwood

A Title IX Trailblazer Breaks Cultural Barriers Through Basketball

Foreword by Jill Hutchison

Prologue
Introduction

Pat McKinzie-Lechault

Foreword by Jill Hutchison

There was a time when females played basketball for the love of the game – not the scholarship, the media attention, the promise of a pro career. This was a rare breed whose passion was usually reserved for their male counterparts. These were the pioneers.

Truly gender cannot dictate one's love of sports, and Pat McKinzie-Lechault bucked the norm through her early years when there were no opportunities for females. She found a way to play in the gyms of her coaching grandfather, father and best friend. She honed her game on what each of them taught her, both on and off the court. Pat, and many others, were victims of the social rejection of all ages —both male and female. And yet she endured, in fact flourished.

Pat's journey is special because she also experienced vastly increased opportunities and the acceptance of females in sports. She is a "Title IX" athlete! She is a product of federal legislation requiring equal opportunity by gender in educational institutions—a law that drastically changed the face of educational sport opportunities for females. Pat and others, experienced high school, college, pro and international basketball, albeit in its infancy. She paid her dues, both physically and emotionally, so her daughter could experience competitive sport as if it had always been an accepted part of society.

Certainly, there were others who experienced the "before and after" of Title IX. However, Pat McKinzie's story captures the depth of emotion felt by a woman moving in a man's athletic world. It is a must read for anyone interested in how we got where we are in women's sports. We are forever grateful for our pioneer athletes whose passion for the game over-rode social mores of the day to bring much needed change.

To win the game is great.
To play the game is greater.
To love the game is greatest!

Prologue

If you deny a woman's history, you erase her identity. I reveal the athlete's untold story, from the passage of Title IX through forty years of social change. What makes it different from other sport biographies is the voice of a woman who walks the talk, who dribbled the ball and tells the story.

So what? Who cares? Anyone coaching an athlete. Anyone playing ball. Anyone loving a game. Anyone raising a daughter. Anyone chasing a dream.

This is the book I longed to read when I was coming of age. It is a tribute to my parents, my sisters, my coaches, my teammates and my athletes, and all those who fought before me and along side me, so that today no female ever questions her right to be "all that she can be." It speaks for the silent pioneers of the past and salutes our highflying daughters of today.

Introduction

I was born to play basketball, but it seemed to me that God goofed big time by giving me, a girl, the drive to do something that was exclusively reserved for boys. Raised in the United States at a time when participating in women's sport was like partaking of the forbidden fruit, I grew up feeling like a bad girl. As a child, I followed my dad, the boys' basketball coach, around the court dribbling a ball nearly as big as I was. I lived for Sunday afternoons in a musty high school field house where an American flag hung above an orange hoop on a square backboard. Though memories are as deeply ingrained as the lines of my handprint, the distinctions among sport, family, and patriotism blend as one. The greatest honor on earth—standing on center court, hand on heart, singing the national anthem, then shooting hoops in a packed arena—was denied to me. Back then, women and ballgames were incompatible entities, but when no one was looking, I knocked down jumpers in game-winning buzzer-beaters just like a boy. I never imagined girls would one day star in their own Showtime.

In the way that I was once driven to shoot baskets in an icy driveway until my fingers went numb, I have been compelled to document the entry of women into competitive sport.

My fighting spirit and athletic prowess were genetic gifts from a Hall of Fame dad and grandfather, who imparted their "never quit" philosophy on the playing fields of Illinois.

During the Depression, when a personable, poor boy from Dixon, disgruntled with the lack of playing time, told the football coach at Eureka College that he wasn't returning after freshman year, that coach, my grandpa, found him a scholarship and a job and encouraged him to work harder. From radio broadcasting to Hollywood film star, that small town boy went on to become the 40th President of the United States.

My grandpa was the first to admit that Ronald "Dutch" Reagan had more talent as a sports commentator talking to a broomstick in a locker room at halftime, than throwing blocks on the field as right guard during the game. In later years, Reagan recounted with self-deprecating humor, that though he was never the football star he dreamed of becoming, he learned greater lessons on McKinzie Football Field at Eureka College than anywhere else in his life.

"Whatever I am today," President Ronald Reagan announced

on ABC national TV, "I feel Coach Mac had an awful lot to do with it."

I know exactly what he meant. So did my father, who grew up dreaming of training his own team, just like his dad had. As the oldest active coach in the nation during the '80s, Coach Mac's career spanned seven decades. Throughout that time, he shaped the lives of hundreds of young men. And of one woman.

Me.

Like my grandpa, I went on to become a pioneer. My gift was also my burden. I eventually forfeited all—family, friends, and homeland—to play professionally abroad. Only in retrospect could I understand how great my sacrifice had been.

In any memoir, past events may be distorted by time, but this is the truth as I remember living it. However, some names have been changed. I feel driven to reveal this story, not for my own glory, but to honor the long-forgotten trailblazers that empowered contemporary young female athletes.

I am committed to commemorating the anniversary of the passage of Title IX in 1972. That bill mandated equal opportunities for children in public education regardless of race or gender. According to the Women's Sport Foundation since then, high school female participation in competitive sports has increased by 990% and in college by 560%. This changed the lives of women in the U.S. forever, like attaining the right to vote had done. I was there when it all started and my story echoes the voices of the lost generation of trailblazers who paved the way for our alpha daughters of today.

Chapter 1: Tomboy

Wisconsin and Illinois 1957-1967

"Thursday's child has far to go"
Children's Poem anonymous

I was born in a town called Sandwich, bit by a rabid skunk before I lost my baby teeth, and grew up as a feisty tomboy emulating Wilt the Stilt (Wilt Chamberlain), a 7'1" Black National Basketball Association basketball star. With such a peculiar debut, it is no surprise that the little white girl of a modest coach's family turned into a storyteller. Even when I told the truth, no one believed me. Who could believe that tale? But, it is true. At least this is how I remember it.

I was a tomboy during the days when tomboy was a derogatory label. As a kid, I had no clue what it meant because my name was not Tom and I was not a boy. As a 5-year-old, when I came home after another squabble with the neighborhood boys, my dad had to coax me out from under my bed before I could explain what was wrong.

"Billy called me a tomboy!"

"That's nothing to get upset about. It just means you like to play with boys."

His response only set off another gale of tears because even children knew "playboy" was obscene, something to do with naked women and S-E-X, another dirty swear word. And, in my young mind, being a tomboy who liked to play with boys was the same as being a playboy!

I hated to be confined. I was a girl everyone insisted should have been a boy to enable my wild spirit to be tamed on playing fields. Between my brunette pixie hair cut and unlaced tennis shoes was a body made of long limbs that tried to out-race sunsets to the shoreline.

I was the second of four children born to an All-American college football player named James McKinzie and his wife, Lenore Olson, a first generation Norwegian American. Their clan included three little girls—Patty, Susie, Karen—four years apart, and a single boy named Doug. When I wore my older brother's hand-me-downs, people often mistook me for a boy. Secretly I smiled when people said to my mom, "You're lucky, two boys and two girls."

I was at odds with the world, growing up at a time when little girls were supposed to learn to cook and clean, not jump and run. Only in the wilderness of northern Wisconsin was I free to be myself. The trees ignored the demands of society. There I spent summers roaming wild.

My grandparents, Ralph and Helen Elizabeth "Betty" McKinzie, were both teachers who loved kids. In 1952, they bought a lodge on the point of the northern corner of Summit Lake, Wisconsin and turned it into a boys' camp. They named it Camp Ney-A-Ti, which means "Deep in the Woods," in honor of the tribes that once owned the land. Boys, aged 7 to 15, slept in cabins called Blackfoot, Chippewa, and Winnebago.

Once a week, everyone wrapped Indian blankets over their bodies, painted their faces, donned head feathers and ankle bells, tip-toed deep into the forest to the Indian Council, and formed a ring around the totem pole for the pow-wow. Although such reenactments may today be considered offensive, back then my grandma, a very spiritual person, was compelled to instill a respect for the indigenous people and the land that she felt was unrightfully stolen from them.

With his high cheekbones, Grandpa resembled an Indian chief proud, sage, and ageless. He completed the look by taking off his glasses, replacing his baseball cap with a headdress, and assuming his coaching stance. Though Grandpa told me he was part Scottish, part Irish, I told everyone he was Native American convinced that my athletic prowess was inherited from my noble ancestors, the mighty warriors.

During my childhood, organized sports for girls were non-existent, yet the day of the boys' track meet at Summit Lake, Grandma Betty made sure I was on the line. I ran my first race on a winding dirt road lined by a quiet green forest. My heart pounded in my temples, dust clogged my throat, and I inhaled the sweet aroma of swamp water as my skinny legs floated toward the finish line. At the banquet, instead of awarding me the first place—after all, it was a boys' summer camp— Grandma handed me a pink ribbon with OUTSTANDING typed in capital letters. I pressed it to my heart.

I exhausted everyone else, but Grandma understood my unending energy, for her small frame was now bent and pained from her own reckless pace. She had juggled career and family long before professional women were fashionable. In 1939, she had coached one of the rare college women's basketball teams the Wartburg Knighties (Iowa.)

Together we rowed through summers at the lake. At dusk, Grandma and I strolled to the end of the long, white pier. With one hand Grandma effortlessly untied Grandpa's slipknot that held the wooden boat fast against the dock, and with the other she balanced me as I rocked the boat with my excitement. Sitting opposite one another, I'd grasp the oars on the inside and push while grandma locked her hands on the outside and pulled. The squeak of the oars harmonized with the creak of the old hull as we rowed from the shore in perfect synchronization. Where Gram's strength ended, mine began.

When working mothers were an anomaly, Grandma Betty had started her career by stomping through snowdrifts to teach at a one-room schoolhouse. Later she had organized athletic banquets and pep rallies for universities in a dervish of energy and creativity. She wore makeup, corsets and perfume; ever the lady, but a lady with gumption. Though she wrote essays, led debates, and directed plays, her finest script was her own life, starring as a feminine feminist before the role existed.

A rebellious spirit of adventure prevailed within my bloodlines. Luckily, even at a young age, I showed signs of that fierce McKinzie spunk. The summer of 1958 was so hot and dry that pine needles crackled like wrapping paper under foot and the lake was down a foot by the end of August. Due to the drought, the locals warned folks to be wary of wild animals scrounging for food. Everyone was busy closing my grandparents' boys' camp. The usual end of the summer sadness was replaced by joy in new beginnings. My mom had just brought my new baby sister, Susan Elizabeth, home from the nearest hospital in Antigo, seventeen miles from our secluded paradise.

For me, just eighteen months, and for my brother, a little more than 3-years-old, it was just another day to eat sand, splash water, and catch bugs. Doug and I were playing outside the camp's kitchen window, when my grandma heard screaming and rushed outside.

"Bad kitty!" Doug yelled.

"What kitty?" Grandma asked scooping me up in her arms.

"That one," Doug said pointing toward the waddling black tail that headed into the dining room through the swinging screen door.

"Oh, no. It's a skunk!" Grandma shouted as the creature meandered through the main lodge toward the bedroom.

"Shoo! Get!" my great aunt screamed from the bedroom.

"Betty, how do you shoo a skunk?"

Grandma tucked me under her arm and chased the skunk to the corner while Aunt Isabel jumped on the old double feather bed.

"Dougie, run get your grandpa and Daddy in the craft shop," Grandma ordered as the skunk padded back out through the door and toward the kitchen. She left me in my hysterical great aunt's arms. The skunk was in the dining room just nudging the screen door open when Grandma came through the kitchen with a bucket. Grandpa pulled the door open and almost caught a bucket on his head while the skunk slipped out the door and under the dining hall.

My grandma abandoned the skunk hunt to calm me. She took one look at the red welt on the back of my hand and knew we were in trouble. Grandma carried me out to the old truck and drove to Doctor Daley's in Elcho. Doc took one look at the marks on my hand and told her, "Oh no, it bit her! Get back to camp and catch that skunk. It could have rabies."

Meanwhile back at camp, the great skunk debate continued.

"Aren't skunks afraid of people?" Aunt Isabelle asked.

"Yes," my dad, the P.E./biology teacher, explained. "But rabid animals go blind and lose their fear of humans."

"How are we going catch him?" Aunt Isabella asked.

"We'll spray him out with the fogger," Grandpa said. While Grandpa sprayed insect repellent from one end of the lodge, Dad dropped an old wooden nail barrel over the skunk's head when it staggered out from the smoke.

"Now what do we do with him?" Grandpa asked.

"No idea. I'll drive to town and ask Orv." At the sole store in Summit Lake, Dad asked the grocer what to do.

"I'm not sure. Don't reckon anyone round here got bit by a skunk before, "Orv said. "Try the ranger."

The ranger told Dad to call a local doctor, who said to call the Antigo Hospital. Dad slumped onto the stool behind the checkout counter where the old ring-up phone perched on a shelf between the canned corn and the boxed cereal. "The hospital is calling the county health officials to send somebody out. They said we need to shoot the skunk!"

"I got a gun you can use," Orv said, tugging his suspenders.

"I know a lady got bit by a rabid dog. She got those shots and lost her hair," said Orv's wife, "Don't worry, Patty'll be okay."

"Thanks for the gun," Dad said as he walked out and down the worn wooden steps to his car.

My mom was napping with baby Susie in the Fox Cabin, but when she heard a gunshot rip through the silent woods, she jumped up and ran outside, clutching her tiny newborn.

"What's happened?" my mom gasped as she saw a group of men standing in a circle at the end of the dining hall looking at the ground. She saw the dead skunk lying in a pool of blood before Dad saw her.

"Oh, Lenore," he said, putting his arm around and turning her shocked face away from the group. "Let's go inside. I can explain. Patty got bit by a skunk."

"What! Where is she?"

"She's okay; she's inside. But we have to send the skunk's head to the state health department in Madison to check for rabies."

"What if it has rabies?"

"Then she'll have to get shots."

"Aren't those painful? You sure they work right? Our old neighbor said her mother had the shots and shrunk."

"Those are just old wives' tales," Dad assured her.

"What would happen if she didn't get the shots?"

"She'd die."

My family closed up camp and headed back to Illinois where my dad started a new teaching job, in a new town, with a new baby, and a new calamity — rabies.

The test results came back positive, so before he even unpacked a box, my dad drove me to the Sterling Clinic.

"Normally, we give fourteen shots crisscross over the belly, but she's so little we'll have to put them in her back," the doctor said. "I've never administered rabies shots to a child this young."

While my dad held me, the doctor injected a long needle into my tiny back. Unable to move my arms and legs, I threw my head back and forth and screamed.

My mom stayed home and tried not to fret, while neighbors who had come to welcome her to town filled her head with gossip about people succumbing to rabies — one woman knew a lady who lost all her hair, another swore that her uncle's pigment turned blue, but the worst story going round was of the little boy who died from the vaccine.

Every afternoon for the next two weeks, my dad rushed home after school before football practice to drive me to the clinic for my shot. When I'd see him pull up the driveway, I'd jump up and down and babble, "Daddy, Daddy." Even in the clinic waiting room, I'd play on his knees. But as soon as I saw the man in the white jacket approach me, I'd wail. My dad tried to keep my back toward the door, holding my hands and feet still while I sat on his lap, so I couldn't see the doctor and his big needle. But as soon as the cool, hard, metal touched my warm soft flesh, I'd screech in anticipation of the pain that always followed. At the end of the fourteen days, a black and blue X covered my back and another smaller stain of fear marked my heart. But my hair didn't fall out, my body didn't shrink and I didn't die. To this day, men in white coats give me the creeps, which is unfortunate since I would spend inordinate amounts of time around doctors.

After my grandparents sold the camp in 1964, Dad and Grandpa built a little red cabin on the western side of the lake. Summers spent at our family cabin in the Wisconsin Northwoods kept me grounded. There I dangled my feet off of the dock and processed my losses, resting my soul for the challenges ahead. There I ran free in torn blue jeans and my favorite T-shirt with P-A-T typed in black letters on the front. In the shimmering reflection of Summit Lake, I pretended that my shirt spelled TAD and imagined that I was a boy, allowed to throw balls, shoot arrows, and climb trees. I made up stories about the boy named Tad who grew up in the forest sharing blueberries with a family of friendly bears.

At the end of every August, we loaded up the old Rambler and drove south to Illinois. Each year, I cried as I kissed the lake good-bye.

Being denied access to the sports that were my lifeblood created an identity crisis for the daughter and granddaughter of coaches. From the time I was old enough to tie my shoes, I followed my dad and Grandpa Mac around gyms, modeling their young male charges. They taught me to kick a soccer ball at twelve months, dribble a basketball at eighteen months and catch a football at age two.

I was such an agile child, nobody thought to tell me that it wasn't ladylike to play ball games with boys. After all, I looked so natural dribbling a ball, running bases or catching a perfect spiral. Every time my dad played catch with my brother, he also tossed a ball to me.

I grew up in Sterling, a town perched on the Rock River and nestled in the world's richest farmland, with its split-level and ranch style houses laid out in half-mile blocks. Every fifth house had a basketball hoop attached to the garage. Children roller-skated on the quiet blacktopped streets and left bikes unlocked on cement driveways.

At a time in American history when little girls were supposed to play house, cut paper dolls and dress up like princesses, my mom let me be a tomboy. Instead of coveting Easy Bake Ovens, Barbie campers and Tammy dolls, when I wanted a basketball, pop rifle and cowboy hat for Christmas, Mom made sure Santa heard my wishes.

Mom never made me wear hair ribbons; instead, she cut my bangs short and let me march to the beat of my own drummer. When I slid into home plate, swished hoops, and tackled the "man" with the ball in the backyard with the neighborhood boys, she grinned and waved from the kitchen window.

When I fell off bicycles and out of trees, she straightened the handlebars and brushed off the grass and said, "Off you go!"

I was lucky because Sterling was a safe place to grow up. Founded in 1834, it was named for Major James Sterling who helped drive the Native American tribes further west during the Blackhawk War of 1832. Built on the north side of the Rock River, Sterling developed around the lumber trade in the 19th century. In the 20th century, Northwestern Steel and Wire, which used the river for power, kept townspeople employed. Other industries, like Lawrence Brothers' Hardware and Wahl Clipper Corporation grew prosperous.

By the late 1960s the population had grown to about 15,000 and was primarily white working class, but included a small percentage of Hispanic/Latinos and Blacks. Surrounding the town, miles of gold and green fields burst from rich soil. With two cinemas, a civic center, a newspaper, a handful of shops like Woolworth's, Grebner's Shoes, Kline's Fashion Store and a half a dozen cafes, Sterling drew business from surrounding settlements and overshadowed its twin city, Rock Falls, across the river. Yet the number one cultural activity was following the high school boys' sports scene. Even in its heyday, Sterling remained a roundball (basketball) town where so little happened that following the local team was a major event.

In those days fans packed the gym, so I always arrived early to secure a front row seat. While the high school band played "When the Saints Go Marching In," I watched the boys in their blue and gold uniforms burst from the locker room and charge across the polished wooden floor. During the warm-ups, the balls bounced in cadence with the drum's beat. I perched at the edge of the bench, one leg bent forward as if coming out of a starting block, the other foot pushing back against the bleacher. Adrenaline pumped through my veins. Like a cat waiting to pounce, as soon as the ball rolled within thirty feet of me, I shot off the bleachers to retrieve it. Then I fired a chest pass back to my favorite player, a slender guard with Smith emblazoned in gold letters across his white jacket, a Black player whose intensity matched my own. He caught my pass, blew on his fingertips as though the ball singed his hand, and grinned back at me. Surely, if there were such a thing as a God of basketball, he sealed our fate in that instant. Destined to come together in the glory of a game we both adored, little did I know that Phil Smith would become my coach, my mentor, and my friend.

But that was later—much later. At the time, I considered it a victory if I even touched the ball during a warm-up.

The change of games marked the seasons of my life. When the leaves turned red and orange, I ran the down and out, the buttonhook, or the slant, clasping the pigskin in my long, nimble fingers. After the first frost, I played one-on-one, two-on-two, or all alone—dribbling, shooting and driving with imaginary teammates at the neighbor's basket. When the snow covered the driveway, I tossed a ball against the basement wall. When the leaves budded and lilacs bloomed, the bat cracked and a hardball smacked as it hit soft leather. And when the sun baked us on long summer days, we hung out on the curb by the orange fire hydrant until bedtime.

Childhood was the time for all sports. And I believed the entire great outdoors was my playground until my eleventh birthday when I sensed my life was doomed as I entered adolescence. Suddenly at puberty, the earth shifted beneath my feet, and my tomboy self fell through the cracks of society.

Chapter 2: Wannabee or Warrior

Sterling, Illinois 1968-1975

"No person in the United States shall, on the basis of sex, be excluded from participation in, be denied benefits of, or be subjected to discrimination under any education program or activity receiving federal financial assistance."

These are the words of the law known as Title IX, which President Nixon signed on June 23, 1972. Its regulations were to be final by July 21, 1975, with full compliance required by 1978.

"Who am I?" I wrote in my diary as an 11-year-old. I remained stuck on that existential question. As a child, I had no role models or parameters to define women starring in an arena reserved for males. I never outgrew the elementary school label "tomboy." In high school, classmates exacerbated my identity crisis by calling me "Wilt the Stilt" to acknowledge my basketball playing prowess.

Throughout childhood, school bored me, but I loved to read. I searched the library shelves, in vain, for books about female heroines, girls like me, who felt more comfortable in blue jeans on ball fields than in dresses at tea parties.

My first hero was Harriet Tubman, who risked her life leading others to freedom on the Underground Railroad. My aspirations were not so grand—I just wanted to play sports—but I admired her strength and fighting spirit

I earned straight A's, but grew weary of the label teacher's pet, so I learned to play dumb to fit in. Tall, smart, athletic with three strikes against me, I slumped through high school.

Whereas other girls fussed over hairdos, nail polish and boyfriends, I spent hours playing ball, writing stories and trying to figure out who I was by understanding my past. Though my mom was a first generation Norwegian American, the only Norwegian I learned was from memorizing the words painted in Rosemaling, on two kitchen wall hangings. One plaque said, *Takk for maten* (thanks for the meal) and the other,

Vaer so god (you are welcome). I swore some day I would visit Norway, the birth land of my grandfather, who died before my mom's 18th birthday, a man I never had the chance to meet.

Movement was inherent in my bloodstream; I was destined to be a pioneer. My forefather, Collin McKenzie emigrated from Scotland in 1655, settling at St. Clement (Maryland) located up the Potomac River at the mouth of Wicomico, as one of America's First Families.

Given my ancestry, it should come as no surprise that I loved to travel. At the turn of the century, the paternal and maternal branches of my family were on the run; some higher force would bring together two separate peoples from across the continents.

In 1902, the same year my Great Grandpa McKinzie's clan moved further westward to Oklahoma, a young Norwegian, Johan Alfred Rosholt, set sail westward across the Atlantic. Unable to live off potatoes in the barren soil in the far reaches of the northern hemisphere, Johan and his son, 6-year-old Edward, immigrated to the Land of Opportunity in search of work. A few months later, his wife, Eugenie, and daughter, Dagny, arrived at Ellis Island on September 2nd. Like so many stories of immigration, the great dream turned to a nightmare. After passing inspection at Ellis Island, Dagny, weakened from the voyage, became ill and died on September 22nd, 1902, a fortnight after arriving on American soil. Three and a half months later, Eugenie, pierced by labor pain, was admitted to the Cook County Hospital in Chicago. On January 25, 1903, minutes after baby Martha Rosholt safely entered the new world, Eugenie left it. Grief-stricken Johan sunk into major depression and returned to Norway. Without a mother to nurse the new baby, and unable to cope, Johan was forced to leave Martha behind. She became a ward of the state and was placed in the Chicago Children's Home. When she was four years old, my grandma Martha was adopted by a Norwegian family, Anne and Alric Raymond.

My Norwegian paternal grandfather, Gustav Olson, grew up on the family homestead in Forra, near Narvick. He lost his mother, and within the span of four years, mourned the passing of three siblings to the Spanish Flu. In search of a better, perhaps happier life, he immigrated to America in 1926 and settled in Chicago to raise a family. Martha met Gustav through family friends. They married on October 29, 1929, the day the stock market crashed.

Though my mom was raised by kind, soft-spoken Norwegians, the impetus to assimilate in the 1940s led to the loss of her mother tongue. Gustav never returned to his homeland. In 1952 at age forty-eight, he died suddenly of spinal cancer just months before his younger sister, Borghild, had saved enough earnings to come see him from Norway. My Grandma Martha was overwhelmed with grief over the loss and daunted by the task of raising a 7-year-old son and putting two older children through college. That, combined with her inability to write Norwegian, led to a severance of ties with our family overseas.

As I thought about my family, a restless spirit coursed through my body. I was the descendent of Scottish lords and Scandinavian ship captains lost at sea. I come from hardy stock, hardworking, law-abiding folk who fought for what they believed in – family, freedom and equality. My ancestors were Civil War heroes; children of sharecroppers struggling to make a living with their bare hands on American soil and Norwegian immigrants seeking a better life. I was the paternal granddaughter of a legendary college coach and a woman ahead of her time. I was the maternal granddaughter of a survivor, my Grandma Martha Olson, who lost her mom the day she was born.

Dealing with loss was as much a part of me as my will to win, yet perseverance was ingrained in my ancestry. And a good thing, too, because at times I felt at war with the world.

"Come on, play you one on one," the boy dressed in his practice shorts and school T-shirt, taunted.

"Okay. Make it, take it," I said, "I shoot first for outs."

The only way I could beat a boy twice my size was to start on offense and make every shot. He checked the ball; I faked a drive right. When his weight shifted forward, I pushed off my left foot and blew by, scoring a lay up.

"Check it," he said as he tossed me the ball.

I faked right, when he leaned to stop the drive, I stepped back and swished a jumper at the top of the key.

"Check," he called as he slammed the ball at my chest. I leaned right. When he overplayed that side, I faked and drove left, laying the ball up with my left hand.

He gritted his teeth and hurled the ball at my ankles. I cocked the ball between my arm and hip and hid my grin by wiping the sweat off my lip with my free hand. I resumed my place at the top of the key, slicing the lane right and left and right again, waiting for his mistake. He stopped my drive right, so I reversed left and hooked the ball over his extended arms.

I made eight straight shots before missing, gaining the psychological edge. He took the ball out and drove to the right. I stepped in front of him as all 200 pounds barreled toward me. "In your face," he taunted as he jacked up an off balance shot. As soon as he released the ball, I threw my hips into him on the block out, gaining a split second advantage to grab the rebound. I dribbled out past the free throw line and hit another J. He smothered me. I weaseled past the left baseline. He recovered and smashed a hand in my face, but I ducked under and popped up on the other side in a perfect reverse—"game."

"Best out of three," he said. "I wasn't warmed up."

Best out of three—they all said that when I clobbered them cleanly on the first round. I continued playing with apprehension. At 5-foot-9, 120 pounds, overzealous competitors had flattened me at other times.

A shrill whistle interrupted our rematch. A coach came out of the locker room and called the boys together.

"Not bad, for a girl," the coach said, adding the qualifier. I looked down, blushing as though standing at the free throw line naked. Then I took the unspoken cue and stepped off the court, making way for the Warriors. From the sidelines, my blue eyes glared at the boys as they sprinted down the polished wooden basketball floor gliding over the inlaid blue Indian head. A group of girls walked through the gym giggling.

"Want to go to McDonald's?" a classmate asked.

"No, I've got homework," I lied, unable to explain that I'd rather stay in the gym.

As a child, except for the Sundays when I followed my dad around the high school gym, begging to shoot hoops, I never envisioned that girls would one day step on the hallowed floor of Sterling High School's Musgrove Field House. I grew up on the sideline, watching my dad's boys' teams.

In the seventies, no one understood a female who felt most at home on a hardwood court, an arena considered forbidden. I slumped against the bleachers to watch the boys practice. No matter how often I won the one-on-one, I still ended up losing.

Fortunately, my dad and grandpa ignored my gender and saw me only as an athlete. Whether I was throwing a football or dribbling a basketball, my dad and grandpa were there with pointers. "Get your head up, knees bent, arm out; protect the ball." When other kids were just learning how to catch a ball, I was mastering the game. My life revolved around the games I couldn't play. Our days were rearranged to accommodate the coaching men of the family. My mom and grandma prepared late dinners after football and basketball practices and games. We made trips to Eureka every autumn to watch my grandpa's Eureka College football team. As my sisters and I cheered, "Go Red Devils" on the sideline, we giggled with delight at the small private Christian college's incongruous nickname.

I grew up as one of the guys, chosen first in pick-up games because I could beat any boy, but gradually the boys matured and felt uncomfortable around me. In the late '60s, tomboy was taboo. Excluded from the boys' world of sports and the girls' universe of dates, my adolescence was doubly painful.

Before my dad's sophomore boys' team practice, I challenged players to one-on-one duels. As I drove the baseline, scoring a reverse lay up against one of the guys, another player would tease, "Hey, Jonesy, where's your jock strap?"

"Ooohh, there it is!" his teammate said pointing up, "hanging from the rafters."

"Take five laps boys," my dad yelled and waved me over. He slung his arm around my shoulder and ushered me toward the drinking fountain.

"I know you could beat any boy out there," he said, "but you know the rules, girls aren't allowed to play basketball, especially on a boys' team."

"So," I said glaring, "break the rules."

"You can always play in the GAA," my dad said.

"Dad, I want to run. GAA makes us walk!"

The Girls Athletic Association (GAA) fostered a "cookies and tea" social group, which emphasized play days for fun, instead of competition. The role of women in sports was parallel to their role in society. The American Physical Education Association cited scientific evidence backed by the medical field that insisted that girls avoid emotional or physical extremes. Playing in the GAA was a far cry from the competitive demands in the European club system or in the

NCAA college game of today.

During two world wars, while men fought abroad women enjoyed new liberties and flooded the work place; however afterwards, American culture had reverted back to traditional gender roles, relegating women to the sidelines as cheerleaders, beauty queens, and housewives. Girls playing basketball was as farfetched an idea as women becoming engineers, doctors, and CEOs. But riding on the heels of the Civil Rights Movement of the '50s and '60s, the feminist and women's lib movements built momentum, pushing the boundaries of conventional womanhood.

After arguing with my dad about trying out for the boys' team, I trudged home from school and threw my books on the couch.

"I want my own team," I said clenching my fists.

"Kind of like wanting to be a Boy Scout," Mom said.

"I want to build fires and camp out," I lamented. "Dumb old Girl Scouts sell cookies and make potholders!!"

A week later I was still giving my dad the cold shoulder. One evening, while reading, he said to me, "Pat, look at this!" He tore a corner off the newspaper page and handed me a five-line scrap that said Title IX passed.

"So what?" I said after I read it.

"So it means that times are changing. Schools have to provide equal opportunities for girls, including sports. If we don't comply, we will be in breech of the law."

"Should I get a lawyer or what?" I retorted.

"Not yet," my dad said and chuckled. "Let me talk to our athletic director first."

I was finally legally allowed on the court, just after I turned "Sweet Sixteen."

While friends went to the pool to sunbathe and chase boys, I hung out in a stuffy gym and played one-on-one against the Sterling Warrior I'd admired as a child when the high school team played. After graduation from Southern Colorado State College, Phil returned to Sterling to teach PE and to coach. In the summer, he organized a recreational basketball league and made sure that I, the only girl, was allowed to participate.

"I'll play you one-on-one for a root beer," he'd challenge, his brown eyes dancing and a wide grin spreading across his handsome face. I'd grit my teeth, drive to the basket and shoot. The ball hung in the air trapped in front of the hoop by his hand, a giant tarantula coming out of the rafters.

Through the love of basketball our unlikely friendship grew, as two social outcasts found a sense of belonging striving to reach a nebulous goal. For a late bloomer who was ahead of her time, the man with a vision understood her in the way the world could not. Somehow, without even speaking in those afternoon shootouts and one-on-ones, a dream took hold. Unknowingly, we were making a lady pro.

During my sophomore year of school, for the first time in Illinois, girls were allowed to have teams, but we could only have a few scheduled games in each sport. In the fall I played volleyball, but my real love was basketball. In those days, our coach, a woman who never had the opportunity to play competitive anything, knew little about game strategy.

"Run the play," she screamed. "Di, throw the ball in to Chris. Chris dribble once, pass to Pat. Patty let her fly."

As I dribbled the ball slowly up the mid-court, my teammates, dressed in one-piece gym suits with pinnies and canvas tennis shoes, marched down the court like the front line of battle, fanned out on either side of me.

"Get off your fat feet," the GAA coordinator yelled. "Or I'll get out my knitting needle!"

At halftime, my dad met me at the drinking fountain and whispered in my ear, "Bring the ball up faster, take the jumper off the dribble, follow your shots for the rebound."

I scored the next twelve baskets to win the game.

I played pick-up ball in the gym every Sunday with guys and my dad knew my game and my team would improve if he encouraged my teammates to join me. Then, ever the patient coach, Dad taught us how to pass, pivot, pick 'n roll, and play together as a team. We won all three games that year and couldn't wait for the next season to start, even though we had to practice in the cracker box gym in the balcony and play in our two-tone blue, one-piece gym suits.

The conditions contrasted starkly with the boy's facilities, especially in Sterling where wealthy businessmen, like the owner of the steel mill, poured money into athletics. Northwestern Steel and Wire, founded by W.M. Dillon, fueled the local economy. In 1936, his son P.W. Dillon installed electric furnaces and began manufacturing low carbon steel and the business boomed. Dillon's great grandson, Pete, a 1953 SHS graduate and highly successful businessman later founded the Sterling Schools Foundation in 1987 and his donations and fundraising led to the creation of state of the art sport facilities and the Hall of Fame Room at SHS.

The successful high school boys' team has always been a source of community pride. Our cement stadium, built in the 1930s as part of Roosevelt's Works Progress Administration (WPA) government employment, put many college facilities to shame. The football field looked like a putting green while the gleaming wooden gym floor was clean enough to eat off of. Meanwhile, girls were relegated to the tiny "girls' gym," junior high gym or a wrestling room with chalk scoreboards. We never had the opportunity to play a game on our home court.

Sterling High School's stately, red brick building with white pillars was built in the 1940s. "Greasers" (boys with greased-back hair) gunned beat-up Chevys on the street, passing under the arch connecting the field house to the school until the noise vibrated through the brick walls, interrupting classes.

By my junior year the class hierarchy was set. The girl "brains" walked the halls with Einstein-type boys; boogie chicks (party girls) and quail (druggy) boys came late to class. "In" girls, usually blonde dolls, who cheered at games, wore the class rings of the jocks, the boys who starred on the football or basketball team.

On weekends the girls had slumber parties, while boys rode around in a jeep called the Moon Mobile, cruising into town on one way Third Avenue and then back out on Fourth Avenue. "Trouble" meant suspension for silly pranks or breaking curfew. Instead of drug busts and drive-by shootings, news headlines in 1975 read, "Sterling Youths Arrested For Streaking the Football Game."

We were a streaking, freaking, bare-butt generation. Radical social changes from the chaotic '60s continued into the '70s. Amid growing dissatisfaction with government, impeachment proceedings, civil rights unrest, and a growing women's movement, American culture flourished. We listened to the '70s hits, read Vietnam War protest literature, and questioned the status quo, restless but stuck in small-town USA.

"Bullshit," "let's boogie" and "life's a bitch" became standard colloquial phrases. As Watergate kids we came of age after the Vietnam War generation. Our school sucked, our government sucked, our lives sucked. We were non-believers -
— studs, burnouts, freaks, nerds, and rednecks searching for

yesterday's misplaced values in sex, drugs and rock 'n roll. And beer.

I'd never had sex, I feared pot, and I disliked beer; however, I had my own drug. I spent hours in the gym getting high to my own song, the swish of a net and the screech of tennis shoes.

I had no role models of athletic women to admire; I identified with Phil, an underdog who loved basketball, too. Bruised by white society and disillusioned by the war, Phil became a cynic at an age when he should've been filled with dreams of youth. He wore jeans with faded flannel shirts, and an army fatigue jacket. He appalled the administration by telling students to call him "Phil" when the norm was for students to use a teacher's formal name such as Mr. Smith. On the fringe of a society, his old house was a refuge for the wounded souls, survivors of Vietnam.

Phil, the first in his family to go to college, dedicated his life to teaching and coaching at his alma mater. Phil knew how much perseverance had been drilled into my education. He'd played football and basketball for my dad at S.H.S.

Phil taught me the circus moves that would one day become NBA staples during our marathon battles of one-on-one. My dad drilled me in fundamentals on Sunday afternoons. My junior year, girls' teams entered the Northern Illinois Conference. That year, I averaged 17 points and 15 rebounds and led my team to an undefeated conference 15-0. Even though I qualified for the state track meet in the 400-yard relay and 800-yard run, the successful basketball season was the highlight of my year.

The highlight for girls was prom, the high school dance that perpetuates the illusion that the princess meets the prince and they waltz into the moonlight. While friends discussed expensive gowns and handsome dates, I ran laps around the track and shot baskets in an empty gym.

When friends flashed their posed prom pictures, I feigned interest and hid my shame until one day I broke down. I headed for Phil's office in tears. "Now what's bothering you?"

"My friends have boyfriends and love cheering for guys. I hate to watch; I want to play! Boys hang out with me, but never date me. What's wrong with me?"

"Nothing! You are ahead of your time. Boys don't understand girls who dig sports; girls have never been allowed to play before. One day, guys will love girl jocks."

The autumn of my senior year, most girls focused on the homecoming gala. Instead of thinking about the dance, I concentrated on the game. The senior and freshman girls challenged the sophomore and junior girls to a game of powder puff flag football as a preliminary to the homecoming weekend. My sister, Sue, a junior, was on the opposing team. Karen, my little sister, a freshman, was our defensive end. I was offensive receiver and Phil was our coach, uniting a pack of giggly freshmen and street kids, Chicanos, poor whites, boogie chicks and "in" crowd into a team.

Before dreaming of being a basketball star, football was my first love. My childhood is laced with memories of being bundled up in snowsuits with my brother and sisters for road trips to other towns. There, the four of us perched beside mom on splintered, wooden bleachers to admire the boys in blue and gold uniforms at SHS or young college men in maroon and gold at Eureka, where the football field was named McKinzie in honor of my grandpa. I grew up to the background beat of battle hymns, to the sound of the marching bands' trumpets and cymbals crashing, and to helmets and shoulder pads clashing.

I identified with my grandpa, who moved cross-country following his first love, football, leaving the wheat fields of Oklahoma in 1916 to attend college and to play football in Eureka Illinois, making his mark first as a player, then as "Coach Mac" at Eureka College and later at Northern Illinois University (NIU).

Ralph McKinzie, my 5'8," white-haired grandpa did not look like someone who once kicked 55-yard field goals and became known as the greatest little halfback in the history of the Little 19 Conference (all Illinois colleges except the University of Illinois and Northwestern). Later, as Coach Mac, Grandpa coached my dad at NIU where he went on to become an All-American.

My dad and grandfather taught me to throw a perfect spiral and to catch the pigskin when I was five. After seeing me pluck a pass out of thin air in a game of catch in the infield, the head football coach told my dad, "No guy can hang on to the ball like that. I'm tempted to let Pat try out for the team."

He never did, though, so the powder puff game was my once-in-a-lifetime opportunity. The night of the game, stars twinkled in an inky black sky and the aroma of apples filled the frosty air. Dressed in old football jerseys, sweat pants and tennis shoes, we sat on the bleachers in the field house listening to Coach Phil's pre-game pep talk. When he opened the door to the field, we surged forward like a dam breaking loose. I kicked off on the emerald field that sparkled under the stadium lights. Voices buzzed from the packed stadium.

After our defense recovered the ball, the quarterback, my best friend, called the down and out in our huddle. On the snap, I sprinted hard left, then cut right, trying to shake my defenders. The perfect pass jiggled through my hands. Phil called in another passing pattern. I watched in disbelief as the pigskin rolled off my fingers again, and bounced off the frozen turf.

In the second half, we scored on a run. They scored on a passing pattern, tying the mark 6-6. In the last minute, our opponents had the ball on our two-yard line. Our defensive unit held them. With 21 seconds remaining, our offensive unit moved in. I knelt in a three-point stance at the end of the line. Hut 1, hut 2, hut 3.

The quarterback reeled back past our own goal line, while I sprinted along the left sideline. I looked back over my shoulder with arms extended toward the heavens when smooth leather smacked my palms. I tucked the football under my arm, dodged the defense and ran on air 98 yards, the length of the field, toward the goal posts. I spiked the ball into the end zone, sprinted toward the bench and jumped in Phil's arms at the 50-yard line. The team folded around us, chanting.

Karen hugged me with tears in her eyes. Sue, squeezed my hand and whispered, "Even if I could've stopped you, I would've let you go. You looked beautiful striding to the sky."

When the excitement of the game died down, the football captains crowned the King, my friend the football quarterback, and Queen, his cheerleader girlfriend. After the coronation, fans and football players mobbed me. While the queen sat up on her throne, I was down among the people being hugged.

For one moment in the blink of a lifetime I was invincible; for 98 yards I tasted the power and glory of manhood, as the star in the Friday night-lights of American football.

Gradually, without realizing it, girls gained ground. We also had a blue, numbered uniform. We donned the same jersey for every sport, every season, but it beat wearing the one-piece gym suit. At the end of the year, we held our own girls' banquet where we received the highly coveted S letter.

By my senior year of high school, I thought I had it all: an athletic team, good coaching by my dad and Phil, and our small contingency of loyal fans, our moms. Even the thrill of a winning basketball season could not compare to my evening on the field. But the conference championship tournament came close. We were down against Rochelle when something inside me snapped.

"Shoot. Take the girl left," Dad whispered as I bent over the water fountain at the half.

"Give me the ball," I pleaded in the second half. Teammates did, thanks to behind-the-scenes coaching from my dad who whispered tips to the coach at half time, too.

"Let someone else bring the ball up the court, so Pat has time to get down court and set up. Then get her the ball."

One after the other, my teammates fed me the pass. I faked, drove, dribbled, spun and sank shots in a human frenzy with machine-like accuracy. I scored 17 points in the 8-minute quarter to turn the losing game into a conference championship title and I ended my high school career undefeated.

In the early infancy of girls' basketball, our conference was limited to 14 games. A conference title was our equivalent of what would one day become a state tournament. I averaged 25 points and 20 rebounds a game in my senior year. Players to follow obliterated my records in their 33-game seasons, but records were made to be broken.

After the game, we raced around the gym in our stiff, cotton twill uniforms. We practiced in a gym so small we called it "the bathroom." Not once did I hear the jazz band play. Yet, throughout my limited high school career I danced from one end of the court to another to the beat of my own drum. After the final game, my teammates cut down the net, draped it over my head, and folded into a group hug, and the music played on in my head. It did not matter to me that after all those hours of shooting hoops alone, only a handful of fans saw my final performance. I represented my town and school, yet played for my own personal satisfaction, for my own joy in movement.

Pioneer blood. Team sport. American pride. From the national anthem that I never had the privilege to sing, while standing on the center court that I never had the chance to star on, to my democratic country that championed the equal rights I was denied, my feelings of being ostracized grew, developing an endless heartbreaking longing.

I grew up playing beside Sinnissippi Park's sacred Native American burial mounds, spent summers at Camp Ney-A-Ti, and cheered for high school boys enacting the Indian emblem charging to battle. As a feisty, imaginative child, the fighting warrior image left a lasting imprint on my soul.

In a childhood laced with camp lore, Sauk Valley history and proud ancestry, I grew up dreaming of being a golden warrior. That summer, I attended the first girls' basketball camps in Illinois, at Illinois State University (ISU) and Pat Kennedy's basketball camp at the University of Illinois. At the end of each week, I came home with feet covered with blisters and a suitcase full of gold. My teams won the championship, and I won the one-on-one and most valuable player awards. I was finding my niche in a most unlikely place: a sweaty gymnasium where I was proving that I, too, could be a mighty, hardwood warrior.

Chapter 3: Scholarship Star

Illinois 1975-77

"The majority of our staff opposed scholarships. It was a real struggle deciding if we were going to do it or not. In the end, we awarded Illinois State's first basketball scholarship in 1978 to Pat McKinzie."
- Jill Hutchison,
Illinois State Women's Basketball Coach (1970-73,1974-99)
1st President and Co-founder
Women's Basketball Coaches Association

"Hey," I said, "I got next!"

Dressed in a tank top and shorts, with a basketball cocked on my hip and my dark hair pulled into a high, tight ponytail, I glared at the young men running down court in Illinois State University's Horton Field House. After one man hit a jump shot, pumped his fist in the air and shouted "game," the skins' team walked off the court.

"Hey, I called winners."

"Ooo, we'll let you play if you go skins!" one guy said, and his teammates laughed.

Another game started, all male. I returned to the basket with a bent rim in the far corner and knocked down jump shots. Nothing but net. But as soon as the pick-up game ended, I was back on the sideline in their faces demanding, "I got next."

No one took me seriously, but persistence paid off. When a player sprained his ankle and no able-bodied men were left in the gym, I finally got into the game by default.

Before recruiters and TV highlights, women played ball, not to impress college scouts or become media darlings, but for our own entertainment. The only glory we needed was the game itself.

A game played for pure joy—as essential to my well-being as the air I breathed. Long before sport psychologists existed, I entered a state of grace where mind and body merged in what we now call "the zone." I still remember a sultry September night decades ago when a player slapped my hand in front of his "brothers" and said, "Give me five, white girl! Can't jump, but you got game."

That was the ultimate compliment.

The perfect state — body, mind, soul, basketball.

We were non-entities back then. Still are. Nobody knows our names. Today, they call us pioneers, back then they called us queers, fools, nutcases. In an era when everyone believed a woman's place was the home, not the hard court, no one knew what to make of us. What blind faith drove us to keep playing in the face of such scorn?

Unknowingly, we were part of a civil rights movement for female athletes that could only be understood in retrospect because the societal changes were so subtle.

Unbeknownst to me, I was at the right place at the right time; however, because of the modesty of the people involved and the lack of media exposure back then, only decades later did I realize the crucial role Illinois State played in bringing about change for women's rights in sports. This was primarily due to the efforts of pioneers in women's athletic administration.

Dr. Laurie Mabry was the director of athletics for women at Illinois State from 1960 to 1982, and women's basketball coach (1965-1970). She was also one of the founders and former president (1975-76) of the Association of Intercollegiate Athletics for Women (AIAW). She fought for equal opportunities, not only for athletes at ISU, but also on the national level.

"It certainly was a challenging time for me here at ISU as well as in the AIAW," Mabry said, "but Illinois State was well ahead of Title IX back in those days for the Midwest."

Mabry also played an important role in the enactment of Title IX of the Education Amendment into law in 1972 and witnessed first hand the controversy surrounding the mandate.[1]

"That fact that everyone just takes for granted that we have an intercollegiate program for women speaks volumes about what Laurie did to establish that program," Jill Hutchison said. "Where we are now, just tells you how far we've come."

---

[1] http://www.youtube.com/watch?v=CjWP2AqMZ8U

Dr. Phoebe Scott, former Illinois State athletics administrator and a former president of the Division of Girls and Women's Sports (DGWS), now known as the National Association for Girls and Women in Sport (NAGWS), was also well-known on the national scene promoting intercollegiate women's sports. Scott became one of the founding commissioners of the first National Intercollegiate Basketball Championship for Women in 1972.

"In the 1960s, I can remember thinking as a young woman that if sports were so good for boys, developing leadership qualities, then why wasn't it good for girls? So I started trying to find out why we didn't participate," Scott said.

"We had been told for years that women were of a delicate nature, and were not made to participate in heavy activity. To do so would be a problem for their health, in particular a problem for reproduction. And we believed all that!"

Together they played a key role in putting ISU women's athletics on the map. Coach Jill Hutchison became tournament director of the first women's national championship tournament, which was held in Horton Field House. She helped set up the regions and qualification process for the tournament, which opened the door to her work within the AIAW.[2]

"Surprisingly," Hutchison said years later, "the regions we set up in 1971 to 1972 are almost identical to those used in the NCAA today."

Pat Head (Summitt), who became the legendary University of Tennessee women's basketball coach, played in that first national tournament. She felt that it was as a turning point for female athletes because just the fact that woman participated was the beginning of something that would lead to greatness.

Hutchison credits her coaching success to timing. When ISU's leaders entered the national scene fighting for legislation, Jill became a part of implementing almost every change in girls' basketball at the front lines promoting equal opportunities for women. In the late 1960s, as a graduate student at ISU, Hutchison attached electrodes to athletes (one was Melinda Fischer '72, M.S. '75 who went on to become ISU's successful head softball coach) and they played a full

---

[2] http://www.youtube.com/watch?v=JoqmTS8OP9M

court 5-on-5 game. Her research proved that a woman's heart wouldn't explode by running up and down a full court.

"These two student-athletes maintained a high heart rate of 180 beat a minute, easily for 10 to 12 minutes at a time with no ill effects," Hutchison explained.

Though the Division of Girls and Women's Sports (DGWS) opposed any alterations in the rules, Hutchison's research forced them to make a change.

Consequently, the half court game with 6 women to a side (2 defenders, 2 rovers, and 2 attackers limited to one third of the court) was abandoned, except in Iowa and Oklahoma. The faster 5-on-5 full court game became official in the 1970-71 season. As part of the rules committee from 1970-1984, Hutchison became involved in every major change in the structure of the women's game. Named Illinois State's head basketball coach in 1970, Hutchison was a rule maker and under her leadership, I became a record breaker.

In the mid-seventies, choosing a college was simple. After camp, I believed ISU had the best women's basketball program in the Midwest and the best women's coach in the country, Jill Hutchison. No one talked me into or out of my decision. Back then recruiting women athletes was unheard of. I chose ISU on instinct.

Founded in 1857, ISU is the oldest and one of the largest public universities in Illinois. Abraham Lincoln was among the attorneys who drew up the school's charter. As one of the earliest teacher-training colleges, ISU endorsed its motto, which is still honored today: "gladly would he learn and gladly teach." It remains one of the top teacher-training colleges in the nation. But to be honest, back then, I wasn't interested in teaching or learning; I went to college to play ball.

In the autumn of 1975, when I stared across an open field at the 850-acre tree-lined campus, I felt like a dwarf. In the foreground, the silhouette of the tri-towers—Haynie, Wilkins, Wright—stood out against the low, flat, sprawling Horton Field House. In the distance, the lights of Watterson Towers, the tallest dormitory in North America when built in 1968, twinkled among the stars. ISU's skyscrapers contrasted with the Midwest's cornfields, creating the illusion of an artificial land, for kids to go and grow up on empty notebooks and kegs of beer.

I threw my shoulders back and strode across campus

toward my dorm. Then my false bravado faded; I felt so alone. Each step I took into the 12-story dormitory, I shrunk a little more. That night, I curled up in the fetal position on my rollaway bed and pulled a pillow over my head to escape.

Tri-towers, stuck on the edge of campus by the field house were labeled "the zoo" due to the high number of African-American coeds. Unlike the Blacks I grew up with, city Blacks, who had been kicked about by white society, wanted nothing to do with us palefaces. I'd greet the girls on my floor; they'd glare at me. I stopped apologizing for my race by being friendly, but quickly looked away. I soon sensed what Phil had tried to explain to me: outside the safe bubble of Sterling, racial prejudice was deeply ingrained in society, even in the more "liberal" north.

This was the first time I had confronted racial tension. I learned from my grandpa, and my dad that you treat everyone equal no matter what race, religion, gender or walk of life they come from.

During the decade before the Civil Rights Movement in the United States, not long after Jackie Robinson broke the color barrier in professional sports, the undercurrent of racial tension escalated. Even in the more tolerant North, an underlying assumption of separate but equal prevailed. In the law of the land, when it came to gender and race, nothing was equal. But in my grandpa's eyes, no man was better than another. Under Coach Mac's creed, equality was non-negotiable.

In the 1940s, Southern Illinois University Teaching College in Carbondale, the host school for a basketball game against Grandpa's team, refused to let Earl Dryden, Northern Illinois' center, sleep in the dormitory.

"What do you mean my big man has to sleep in the basement?" Grandpa said to the host school's coach.

"School rules. Niggers are not allowed in the dorms."

"Damn it! Then give me a cot," Coach Mac fumed, "and I'll sleep in the basement, too."

My own experience in team sport had also taught me to defend and depend on my fellow teammates, regardless of skin color or social standing.

When I was in college, though animosity may have existed between races when we were outside the gym, on the court inside Horton Field House, Black ball players accepted me far more quickly than the white guys.

In 1970, ISU hired Will Robinson[3] who broke the color barrier among Division I basketball coaches by becoming the first African American head coach. While Hutchison fought to obliterate the myth that full court basketball could kill women, Robinson was shattering stereotypes about African Americans' abilities in the professional ranks. Though he left ISU after the 1975-76 season to work for the Detroit Pistons, he paved the way for African American coaches and guided the college career of U.S. Olympian and NBA star Doug Collins. [4]

After classes, I attacked my training program in the weight room in Horton, across the street from my dorm. Then I ran two miles in the residential area off of the campus, sprinted the stairs up to my room and grabbed my basketball. If I couldn't get into a pick-up ball game with the "brothers," I found an empty corner of Horton where I dribbled lengths of the court and shot baskets until I was too exhausted to think.

I met John in a pick-up game in the gym when he challenged me to a one-on-one match. When I beat him, he laughed. Instead of insisting on a rematch, he asked me out for pizza. In the beginning, unlike other guys I had dated on occasion, though he loved sports, John didn't seem threatened by my athleticism. One date led to another and soon we were inseparable.

During my teens, I never figured out if boys were afraid of me or of my dad, the revered coach. John, from another part of Illinois, was oblivious of my family history, at least in the beginning of our relationship.

John, my first love, shared all my firsts. But even after I had a steady, I wondered why girls fawned so over men. A part of me remained detached, focused on my schoolwork and training in preparation for the basketball season. But he insisted on being together between classes and on the weekends. At first his demands were subtle, so I gave in thinking it was part of the sacrifices one made for a partner. Soon, too much of a good thing turned bad. Though I sensed something was wrong with the relationship, I clung to my security blanket during my freshman year.

---

[3] http://sports.espn.go.com/ncb/news/story?id=3371978

[4] http://www.nba.com/coachfile/doug_collins/

Once the official season started, I had even less time to spend with John. He was also beginning to struggle with his coursework. The greater his dissatisfaction with college life in the general, the more pressure he put on me. He showed streaks of jealousy. Slowly, insidiously the relationship changed. We spent more of our time together fighting and then making up. Sunday nights were the worst. I was haunted by memories of lazy Sundays at home where church followed by roast beef and football were comforting family rituals.

I felt emotionally drained from trying to keep John's spirits up. I hated the cold indifference of the classroom where one hundred anonymous bodies slumped in chairs listening to the monotone of a professor. I disliked the impersonal dorm life. I even dreaded basketball practice. The girls treated me with disdain, except Sal, who chose me on her team and set me up for shots. After practice Coach called me into her office.

"We want to give you a scholarship," my coach said, "but this is the first year scholarships have been awarded in Illinois. To be fair to everyone, you'll have to try out for it with the rest of the team."

"Ok-kay," I stammered.

With four kids only five years apart, my parents struggled to make ends meet on their teachers' salaries. A scholarship would help out. I increased my weights, ran more miles and pushed to exhaustion at practice. I received a letter from ISU's Dr. Laurie Mabry, stating, "you have been selected as a student who should receive an athletic scholarship at Illinois State University."

I was thrilled to be the only freshman selected, yet Sal was the only teammate happy to see me on the squad.

"John, I made varsity!" I said on the phone.

"Good for you, superstar," he said icily. "We should split up! With road trips, we'll never see each other."

John's neediness exhausted me, especially when I felt overwhelmed with college life. He wanted to quit school. I preserved my sanity by playing ball. Since finding a friend, practices went smoother. After practice, Sal asked me out for a drink. I declined.

"Hey, Pat," Vonnie said. "Can we talk a sec?"

I felt honored to be singled out by our point guard.

"I don't know how to explain," she said fidgeting, "the team thought you should know. Sal is gay."

"What?"

"You know, lesbian. It's your choice what you want to do, but we didn't want you to get taken advantage of."

"Geez, Vonnie," I said. "I've got a boyfriend."

"Yeah, we know. See you at practice," Vonnie said flipping her black hair off her forehead and slipping outside.

"Wait, what about road trips?" I called out to her. "Who will I room with? Who's straight?" I dashed outside. An icy wind whipped across the plains slapping my face with a sobering reality: my only ally on the team was gay. At the dorm, I called John for affirmation of my heterosexuality.

Next practice, I cringed when Sal passed me the ball.

"How about Friday night?" she asked after practice.

"No, I'm going out with John."

"Maybe some other time?"

"No," I retorted, looking over my shoulder. Do teammates think I'm her new lover? At a loss as to how to handle the situation, I felt ashamed shunning the only teammate who had been kind to me. In the seventies, we called one another faggots as the ultimate insult, yet no one growing up in small town USA knew any homosexuals personally. In those days, to love one's own gender was as taboo as incest. People attracted to the same gender remained in the closet, under the lock and key of society.

The roller-coaster relationship with John sapped my energy, and, as a result, my confidence in basketball deteriorated. Preoccupied by the unknown sexual inclinations of bunkmates, I scarcely slept on road trips. In the beginning, I started in the line up, but later in the season I saw "pine time" (sitting on the bench). In high school, I'd played every minute and was now unsure of how to adjust to going into the game whenever and wherever I was needed.

Before home games, I glanced behind our bench to see my parents and grandparents in the empty stadium. Grandma cheered, "Go Redbirds," while Grandpa hollered, "Protect the ball!" At half time, Dad met me at the drinking fountain.

"Fake the shot and drive."

"Anything else?" I asked, leaning over gulping water.

"Overplay number 15 right. She has no left."

We matched baskets with Ohio State in the final minutes, but all I could think was "I want this over." At the time out, I spilled the water bottle. Even after the game ended in our victory and we squeezed into the Steak 'n Shake ® booth, my hands still shook.

"Don't hesitate," Dad said, "Get back on D faster."

"Never saw so many bad passes," Grandpa grumbled.

"Want to eat anything?" Mom asked, changing subjects.

"I'm never hungry right after a game."

"Don't be so hard on yourself," Dad said. "You're going to be the first girl ever to receive the Roscoe Eades Award for outstanding athlete at Sterling High. The football coach nominated you. Coaches voted unanimously for you, but decided it wouldn't be fair not to award a male, too. You are setting a precedent."

"I don't feel outstanding now!" I said swirling my milkshake with a straw. "I hate sitting out, but when I get in the game, I'm too scared to play."

"You're the only freshman. You're learning the ropes."

"Sorry I'm down," I said. "I'm glad you came to watch."

"Don't worry about us," Mom said, sliding her arm over my shoulder. "We're happy to see you, win or lose."

"Anyway, Dad, who the heck was Roscoe Eades?"

"He was a highly respected superintendent who did a lot for Sterling schools."

"Roscoe was one of my boys, too," Grandpa added. "Played football for me at Eureka."

After one home game, my parents and grandparents picked me up and we drove through a blinding snowstorm to reach Sterling High School just minutes before the half-time presentation of the Roscoe Eades Award. Initiated in 1961, this was the most prestigious award a high school male athlete could receive. In 1975, I unknowingly ignited a new trend. But when I look back, all I can remember is Grandpa grumbling about the poor visibility driving through a blizzard. My parents would remember it as the night a girl had received a Roscoe Eades award for the first time.

A few weeks later, after we'd won the state championship, I missed the first game of the regional tournament when my beloved Grandma Betty died peacefully in her sleep of a massive stroke or a heart attack. At the visitation, I walked over to the casket. A ray of sunshine sparkled through the stained glass window forming a halo over Grandma's head. "No, Gram, don't leave me," I wept. In church, the pastor praised Grandma's service to mankind. Then, while they drove

Grandma's casket to Augusta to be buried, dad whisked me to the airport. For the first time, I didn't want to play, but after winning the state championship, my team advanced to the AIAW regional's. Dad convinced me that Grandma would have wanted me to participate in the tournament.

So I played. We finished fourth, but as soon as the tournament was over, I couldn't remember even touching the ball. Yet twenty-four hours after the season ended, I returned to the hard court for comfort. After class, I headed to a corner of McCormick gym to shoot. Alone with the ball and basket, I mourned the loss of my number one fan, my grandma, a pioneer in her own right.

Both my mom and grandma were spiritual and as a child I was full of blind faith. But as a young adult, I doubted everything, especially myself. Yet as I drove the baseline, a mysterious force propelled my limbs forward — Grandma was still with me.

Occasionally a cocky guy interrupted my shooting routine and challenged me to a one-on-one match or a teammate wandered in for a round of horse, but most of the time I was alone.

John and I were together on and off during summer, but my heart belonged to basketball. I never wanted to sit on the bench again. Phil would be the first to admit one of the best perks about teaching at SHS was his set of keys to "the castle," the field house. When I wasn't working at the pool, Phil and I dueled in marathon battles of one-on-one under a spotlight on the main court of the hot, musty gym. When he attacked from the foul line, I stopped him, but he twisted up over my arms, toward the hoop. I'd drive to the hole, and as a big black hand flew in my face, I'd see the ball come crashing back at me.

"Put it back up! I can block you once, but not twice."

In the middle of our workout, I'd call "water break" and brush away tears at the drinking fountain. But I learned about second effort that summer.

"I found a camp for you to go to," Phil said.

"They don't have girls' basketball camps in the area."

"I know — it's a boys' camp. Lee Frederick's one-on-one."

Phil went with me the first day and made sure they would let me participate. I lined up behind the boys who were a head-and-shoulder taller and 50 pounds heavier than I was. I learned how to dribble behind my back and between my legs. I learned how to spin and developed the skyhook. I got beat playing one-on-one against the guys, but I never quit. At the end of the week, when the boys took home their medals and trophies, I left with my bruises and a bunch of new moves to practice. For the rest of the summer, my dad helped me with the fundamentals and pushed me to perfect my jump shot while Phil helped me master the new moves. In the mornings he taught me "Kareem's skyhook," a blind flip-shot over the shoulder, requiring perfect touch. And I mastered power drives. In the afternoons, I worked at the pool and swam laps during my break. At night, I played ball with guys.

At the end of the summer, I went to ISU basketball camp to work as a counselor. Between sessions, we played semi-organized games.

"Girl, whatcha been doin'?" said Charlotte Lewis, our six-foot-three, one-hundred-eighty-pound All-American Black center. "I can't stop ya no more." The day I beat Charlotte one-on-one, I knew I'd earned my position.

My sophomore year, along with my classes, I had a strict, self-imposed work-out schedule including weight training, running, and individual shooting workouts. Vonnie often joined me in the gym at night when we challenged boys to pick up games. In the beginning, we had to fight to get on the court. The standing rule was winner stays on and anybody can pick a team to challenge. Vonnie would call the next game and while we waited, we'd search for the three biggest, baddest guys to complete our team. At first the guys laughed at us. After we pulled up short for a shot and taunted, "count it" as we swished shots, they took us seriously. By the end of our first month back on campus, we'd earned our rights on the courts with the boys. Some of the brothers even picked us on teams by asking, "Hey girl, wanna run?"

With new friendships, including my new roommate, my need for John decreased while his need for me grew greater. As if he sensed I was drifting away from him, he clung to me, destroying whatever love was left. One night I arrived home from practice to find John waiting for me. He said he needed to talk. When he got to my room he accused me, "You love basketball more than you love me."

"Don't be silly; you can't compare the two things."

"Would you give up basketball if I asked you to?"

"No way. Basketball is paying for my education."

"You would never give it up, you're a scholarship star on a big ego trip." John grabbed the new ball off my desk and slashed it with his pocketknife.

"What are you doing? That's a leather ball you're ruining." I took a step toward him as he threw the deflated ball.

"What in the hell is wrong with you?" I hollered.

"You're the sick one, you and your gay team."

"We're not all gay. If you loved me, you wouldn't ask me to choose."

"Well, I am asking. What's your choice?"

"Basketball," I screamed. As I stepped toward him, his hard fist connected with my face. My head snapped back. "Get out," I yelled, trembling. "Out."

"Oh, God, I'm sorry, Pat. I don't know what I was doing."

"Get out! Now!" I shouted pushing him away.

When he left the room, I locked the door, sat on my bed and when I was sure he was gone, I slipped down the hall to the bathroom and held a cold washcloth to my right eye.

"What happened to you?" friends asked.

"I caught an elbow in practice," I joked, determined to break up with John. What if everyone else believed, like he accused, that I was gay because I loved basketball?

After the violence, John was gentle. We were continuing part of the vicious cycle of fighting and breaking up, then kissing and making up. Now we were destroying each other.

"Why do you always put basketball first?"

"Basketball is my priority. It pays for school. They're giving me a full ride."

"I'm sick of being second best. Find another boyfriend."

"Good, I'm sick of this sick relationship."

John grabbed my T-shirt by the neck and pulled his fist back. I saw what was coming and jerked away. My shirt ripped in half. "Get out!"

"I'm sorry, Pat. I didn't mean it. I need you."

"We can't go on. We're destroying each other. I'll still help you with your schoolwork. I can't take the fighting any more."

"If that's what you want, but I'll always love you."

The next day, in chemistry class, John slid into the empty seat beside me. He sent me pictures of a stick man hanging himself. Underneath the stick man he wrote, "John."

"Stop it," I insisted. "Stop this silly hang man game."

"It's no game. If you leave me, I'll kill myself."

Even though I broke up with John by Thanksgiving, he continued to play mind games and threaten suicide. When he called in desperation, I tried to calm him down, but my role had changed from that of a girlfriend to a counselor. While John threatened to take sleeping pills, drink Drano and destroy both of us, Phil's open arms offered me a chance to grow up and go on wherever life would take me. With a big squeeze and a hard shove, Phil pushed me off into the next adventure.

Over Christmas during our five-day break, Phil and I picked up where we left off back in the gym, perfecting the jump shot, honing the drive. In the evening I'd hang out at his place, a way station for all the lost souls in Sterling.

"Hey, run it down," he'd grin from ear from underneath his mustache as guests stepped through his unlocked back door. I'd sit back and listen to their laughter and banter that mixed with Smokey Robinson's mellow sound. Sometimes when a woman friend arrived, I'd take my unspoken cue to leave. Other times when the last friend had driven away, Phil would ask, "What's up? You seem down."

My troubles melted away as I talked about my insecurity about gays, my fights with John, his destructive dependence, and my uniqueness from friends.

"I'm just so different from everybody else."

"What's wrong with that?"

"I feel like an outcast."

"Everybody feels that way sometimes. You are different. Nobody else looks, thinks or acts like you."

"What if I'm gay, because I love basketball so much?"

Phil smirked until he saw the tears in the corner of my eyes, "Whatever gave you that idea?"

"John says I'm gay because basketball is the only thing that matters and I hate kissing John now."

"That doesn't mean you are gay. That only means you don't love John anymore. Feelings you had for him are gone. You'll always love basketball. I love basketball and I'm not gay."

"But you are a guy. Guys are supposed to love basketball. And John's always telling me."

"Pat, quit listening to John. You've outgrown him. Go on, get on with your life. Don't look back. Just let go."

In the gym, he'd peel off his sweats to his form-fitting T-shirts and shorts that flattered his supple, strong muscles. When we played one-on-one, I'd shoot and go hard for a rebound, but he blocked out, preventing me from getting the ball. With teeth clenched and muscles taught we battled it out in the gym where we shared feelings in the only acceptable way. We shared an elusive feeling expressed in a love for the game, trapped in our one-on-one world.

As a sophomore, though, I was technically still a rookie; my upper-class teammates made me look good. With Cindy Ellis and Cyndi Slayton, giving us senior leadership, and juniors Charlotte Lewis at center, Vonnie at point guard, and me at left wing, we became a powerhouse.

Charlotte was the key to our success. She could out-rebound men and dunk the ball in practice. However, the media barely registered that women's basketball had been added as an Olympic event for the first time in Montreal 1976, let alone mentioned that Charlotte and her USA team earned a silver medal. Pat Head (Summitt), who later became the college game's most decorated coach, co-captained that first United States national basketball team. But back in the '70s, nobody made a fuss, least of all Char.

In February Phil came down to film a game on his 8mm reel to reel. After the game, for the first time ever, we went out together outside of the gym, but even strangers acted offended. At Denny's, no one would wait on us.

"It's always like this," Phil said glaring at the waitress. "She won't wait on us because we're together. And the white guy won't serve us either."

"It's because it's so late," I said. "They're tired."

"Pat, do you see anybody else eating in here? No, the place is empty. They are not too busy or too tired. I know what I'm talking about. See how the world would treat us."

"I'll go up and tell them what we want."

"We're not begging for service. Let's go."

I walked out of the place, with a growling stomach and a heavy heart.

Phil, understanding we were playing with fire, kept his distance in public. "Down in Alabama they'd lynch a man for looking at a white woman." I thought he was paranoid until thirty years later when I was teaching my international students about slavery and the Civil Rights Movement through revised history books that included the reality of the past. I saw that racism was indeed ingrained into the social fabric of America. Until the Supreme Court shot down miscegenation laws in 1967, Blacks and whites could not legally marry each other in sixteen states. Even decades later in the liberal North, interracial relationships were discouraged.

My ISU team had a 20-6 record playing against Big Ten schools, going into the Association for Intercollegiate Athletics for Women (AIAW) Large College State Championship at Northern Illinois University. As the second leading scorer, with an average of 14 points per game, I came into my own at the state tournament, pumping in 25 points against Chicago Circle and another 22 points against DePaul before beating Northwestern in the final.

Our euphoria over our victory was short-lived when we were upset in the regional at Purdue, and lost our chance for the nationals. Two days after the defeat, I returned to the gym, running and shooting — training for the next season.

I secretly dreamed of making the Olympic team. I came closer than I ever imagined possible.

After my sophomore year at Illinois State, during summer camp, my coach told me that I was invited, along with 24 other girls to try out for the 1977 World University Games, which is preparation for the Olympics. She explained that the selection committee would pick 12 players to represent the USA in Sofia, Bulgaria, in August.

"Here's your ticket to New York," she said. "You've got a good shot at it."

"Thanks," I mumbled, too dumbfounded to speak. I had no idea who paid for the flight. Knowing Coach, she probably took it out of her own meager coaching salary.

"The try-out camp will be held at New York State University at New Paltz. Better get your passport ordered."

I thought it was a once in a lifetime chance. What I didn't realize was the opportunity was so new for any girl: 1976 was the first year Olympic medal competition for basketball for women existed. Charlotte starred in that final, a match-up between the USA and the powerhouse Russia.

I returned from camp and began the necessary paperwork. Phil put in extra time with me at the gym. I had only ten days to prepare.

Charlotte took me under her wing, and we roomed together in New York. In the gym, we met our competitors. I knew all their names: Rita Easterling, Mississippi; Nancy Lieberman, Old Dominion; Pat Roberts, Tennessee U.; Carol Blazejowski,

Montclair State, NJ; Nancy Dunkle, California State U.; and Annie Meyers, the highest profile and arguably best guard in the nation. Lucille Kyvallos (Queens College) and Dixie Woodall (Oral Roberts) were the well-known coaches.

As soon as I walked into the gym and saw all the big names, I felt beat. I was so nervous when we had to run plays that I couldn't even remember the right and left side of the court. The coach kept yelling "shoot," because she knew that was what I did best, but every time I got the ball, I froze. As soon as I released a shot, I jerked my arms back as though it was a mistake. Without my natural follow-through the ball flew hard against the rim or backboard. At night I couldn't sleep. I just wanted it to be over. After just a day and half, I was sitting on the bench. With little playing time, every second I was on the court, I felt I had to prove myself. My shots and moves were no longer smooth and fluid. I became a jerky robot. Even though I was still in the last fifteen, I was relieved when they told me I could fly home. I was one of the last ones cut, but all I could think of was how terribly I'd played. I beat myself. My parents were full of encouragement when they picked me up at the airport. I hid my anguish until I got home. Then I went into the basement, threw myself on my bed and sobbed. I thought I'd never have the courage to go out that door again.

Sue tapped at the door, "Can I come in?" She sat on the bed. "Next year you'll be even stronger. You can try out again."

"I'll never try again," I said, slumping into her arms.

"Yes, you will; you're a fighter and," the phone interrupted her. "Just a sec," she said into the receiver. "Pat it's for you. It's Phil."

"No, I don't feel like playing," I shouted into the phone. "No more basketball. Ever. Again. Don't you dare mention the B word again."

Chapter 4: Sisters Win First State Championship

Illinois, April 1977

"I am a huge believer that sports end up being good for kids, and especially good for girls. Studies show that girls who are involved in athletics often do better in school; they are more confident in terms of dealing with boys. For those of us who grew up just as Title IX was taking off, to see the development of women's role models in sports, and for girls to know they excelled in something, there would be a spot for them in college where they weren't second-class, I think has helped to make our society more equal in general," President Obama said.

"I think the challenge is making sure that, in terms of implementation, schools continue to take Title IX seriously... and I think understanding that this is good, not just for a particular college, not just for the NCAA, [but that] it is good for our society; it will create stronger, more confident women."[5]

In 1892, a year after James Naismith invented the game of basketball for men; Senda Berenson adapted the rules for women. Illinois also played a historic role. On December 18th, 1896, Oak Park High and Austin High played the first known women's interscholastic contest. Over 300 Illinois high schools sponsored girls' basketball teams by the time the Illinois High School Association (IHSA) was founded in 1900 and the first state basketball league was formed. The initial boys' state tournament was held in 1908.

In spite of the growing popularity of girls' basketball with students and by the press, school administrators backed by the academic community condemned what they considered the masculinization of female athletics. The fact that girls played ball by boys' rules, sometimes against boys' teams, on teams coached by men and in front of boisterous crowds of boys, infuriated administrators.

In 1907, the Chicago Public Schools Superintendent, Edwin

---

[5] http://espn.go.com/espnw/title-ix/7737386/espnw-title-ix-president-obama-discusses-importance-title-ix

G. Cooley forbade city teams from organizing its girls' basketball league. A year later the Illinois High School Athletic Association banned girls from participating in interscholastic sports, especially basketball.[6] The nationwide backlash against girls participating in interscholastic sport followed suit. This led to the demise of girls' basketball programs in Illinois, a movement that was followed in the rest of the nation.[7]

Ironically, Illinois, where the first girls' high school game was played, fell far behind when the people in power, swayed by the social climate of the time period, decided that basketball was unhealthy, unfeminine and unwanted in the state. It wasn't until 1972 that Title IX forced the issue reversing this trend. Almost a century after Chicago Public Schools banned girls' basketball leagues, the first girls' high school championship was held in Illinois on my college campus.

My own family athletic history was intricately tied to the state and an Illinois boy, who went on to become the President of the United States. In his college coaching career, my grandpa shaped the lives of hundreds of athletes, including Ronald Reagan, who played at Eureka College from 1928-1932. Grandpa was famous for the "never quit" attitude he instilled in his college football players.

"Ever heard of the duck walk?" the President chuckled as he recounted one of those character-building lessons he learned while playing for Coach Mac. "He used to make us squat down on the end line and waddle across the field. Just when we were about to drop at the opposite goal post, Mac would yell, 'c'mon back.' When you played on Mac's team, you learned to do things beyond your strength."

Another not-so-famous player, who held my grandpa in the highest esteem, was my dad. My dad once held the national pass receiving record for small colleges. He lettered in three sports at NIU back in the day when college athletes could compete in more than one discipline. Of all his accomplishments, what made him proudest was playing ball for his dad. It wasn't always easy because Coach Mac set such

---

[6] http://www.ihsa.org/

[7]

http://www.ihsa.org/NewsMedia/IllinoisHStoric/IllinoisHStoricArticle.aspx?url=/archive/hstoric/basketball_girls_early.htm high standards, but my dad's admiration for his father was genuine. From the time he was a little boy, he knew he wanted to grow up to be like Coach Mac. After my dad earned his master's degree, completed military service, and his first teaching job at Somonauk, he was hired at Sterling where he remained ever loyal to the blue and gold. He coached year round, all sports, but his greatest love was basketball and he coveted the head coaching position, biding his time, as the loyal assistant coach. When the head coach retired, my dad applied and got the job. He inherited a troubled program. For two years prior, he had held the team together by preventing athletes from quitting and by counseling players who had no respect for the head coach. I burst with pride, swaggering in the halls of Challand Junior High on game days and lost my voice from cheering on Friday nights. But something was amiss. My outgoing, cheerful dad stopped whistling. He became withdrawn and preoccupied, as an ulcer ate away at his stomach lining. Ill and anxious, trying too hard to please everybody, he resigned to save his health. But God had other plans. He began coaching me on Sundays. A few years later, the girls' coach invited him to share the bench with her. The team gleaned valuable insight into the game from his expertise. Yet, ever modest, he will play down his own role in making history.

Five years after the Title IX law passed, the Sterling Golden Girls, the high school team that Sue Strong, my dad, and Phil coached, qualified for the first-ever girls' state basketball tournament.

In the early infancy of women's sports, with a negative stigma still attached to female athletes, team names were feminized. Instead of the mighty Warriors, Sterling female counterparts became known as Golden Girls. However, no one on the team felt that the title was demeaning; they were too proud to be wearing the blue and gold to care what anybody called them.

On April 1st, 2nd, 1977, the last vestiges of Old Man winter whipped across Illinois State's campus, but Horton Field House, packed with thousands of pulsating fans, felt like a sauna.

A shrill whistle interrupted the action at center court. The girls in gold uniforms rushed to the sideline to huddle around my father, Phil and Sue. A minute later an official beckoned the players back on the floor. A girl with my hair and eye color, wearing my number, went to the free throw line as I watched from the bleachers. She glanced at the scoreboard. Two seconds remained; she only needed one. She dribbled twice, spun the seams straight, and then released the ball from her fingertips with a perfect backspin. I held my breath as number 23, ace shooter Karen McKinzie, stood at the line poised to upset undefeated Chicago Fenger, the dynasty in Illinois basketball. Only she missed. No one could believe it. Especially not my sister. "It felt so good when I let go," Karen later told reporters, "I was sure that I made it."

The game went into overtime. "When I saw Karen at the line alone to seal the win," my dad said, "it was the first time I thought of her as my daughter, not as a player."

After the missed free throw, the team gathered in the huddle looking devastated. My dad, with years of coaching experience, acted as if he had written overtime into the final script. "Great! We'll show fans that the girls' game is as exciting as the boys. Dig deep. Take it to them in overtime!"

Co-captain, Marche Harris, leaped three feet high as she left the huddle cheering and leading the team back onto the court.

Karen scored 20 points in the victory as Sterling went on in overtime to upset the undefeated Chicago Public League powerhouse, Fenger. Sterling spectators stormed the players. Doug, ever the big brother protecting his little sister, spread his arms out as if to stop the sea of fans from flooding the court.

"Every opponent was a mystery," my dad said. "There were no scouting reports, so you had no idea of the competition. You went into every game cold turkey and made adjustments as it progressed."

"After we beat Fenger in the first game, it dawned on me that I had better stay and scout the next game because we would play the winner."

Next Sterling beat Fremd. Then my dad's coaching knowledge gave the Golden Girls an edge. He threw a full court press on Washington High School in the final to shake things up; Washington never really got back in the game.

For two days, my old teammates had battled their way to stardom in front of thousands of ecstatic hometown fans. Eshelman, Harris, Leseman, McKinzie, and Smith are family names that marked Sterling High School record books for years. Karen's missed free throw would be forgotten; instead, her name would be engraved forever as the first player introduced and the scorer of the first basket in the first Illinois girls' state high school basketball tournament.

Late that night, the girls drifted to sleep with gold around their necks and special team mascots, Cookie Monsters, clutched in their fists. My mom had dressed the stuffed toys in hand-stitched yellow jerseys bearing each player's number, and given one to each girl.

When the team drove back to Sterling in a caravan of cars, the entire town lined the streets to greet them in an unofficial parade. A fire truck, a police car, and thirty carloads of fans greeted them at the junction of Illinois Route 88 and U.S. Route 30 at the south edge of Rock Falls. The convoy escorted the triumphant team to the Sterling High field house where another 3,000 fans jammed the gym for a celebratory assembly. Neighbors stood on their porches, cheering and waving signs. East 19th street had a sign on either end of the block announcing to all who drove by that they were "Entering Golden Girl Territory."

During the following week, the Sterling Golden Girls were the toast of the town.

"So many local restaurants invited us for free meals," Frannie said, "I must have gained ten pounds!"

The Golden Girls put Sterling on the map. The whole community celebrated the success, a state championship. A group of unassuming, charismatic girls brought new life to a community that had been struggling. At the Rotary Club luncheon, they were the only women in the building. The team appeared on the Ray Raynor show in Chicago. State Representative Cal Schuneman invited the Golden Girls to Springfield for a tour and to meet-and-greet with Governor Bill Thompson.

Until this event, girls played sports in obscurity, without recognition and without the help of a full coaching staff. Even teams that had a 22-0 record like the Sterling Golden Girls rarely received attention—even from their local newspaper or radio station, so the spontaneous outpouring of media interest was unprecedented.

On April 4th 1977, The Daily Gazette headlines read, "Over 7,000 greet Illinois' number one Sterling High School girls' basketball team." Five years after Title XI passed into legislation (1972) mandating equal opportunities for girls in schools, a new generation was born. While America still reeled over civil rights and gender equity, a small town team spontaneously united Blacks, whites and Hispanics in one dream—a state championship.

Marche Harris usually pumped her fist after a break away lay up. Center Fran Smith (Coach Phil's sister) towered above opponents with her three-inch Afro hairdo. Solid Dawn Smith positioned herself for weak side rebounds while Jojo Leseman ran the court like a platoon captain in fast forward. Freshman Amy Eshelman glided the baseline and Karen swished free throws in perfect form. Elva Fuentes, the 5'3" team manager, inspired the players with her endearing chatter of support as she filled water bottles. A strange mix of coaches guided those golden girls: Jim McKinzie, a former boys' coach, Sue Strong, a GAA coordinator who never had the opportunity to play competitively, and Phil Smith, the first African American teacher in the Northern Illinois conference. In those crucial years after Title IX, with the support of athletic director, Bob Henard, they fought behind the front line to ensure female athletes received equal rights at SHS. Before anyone dared utter words like racism or sexism in public, the odd trio of a white father (Karen's), a Black brother (Fran's), and a determined woman created a team that was far ahead of its time in its indifference to race or gender.

It was too late for me to star in high school basketball, but I had paved the way for them. As a 1975 SHS graduate, I had moved on to ISU. At the first-ever girls' state tournament, held on my new home court at Horton Field House, I watched with pride and more than a little envy as my little "sisters" made history under my father's tutelage.

"What stands out most is not the games, I was too caught up in the play by play, but how this team brought the community together," my dad said. "The Golden Girls were goodwill ambassadors for Sterling, the place that no one had heard of before was now suddenly stealing the limelight. When we returned home from State, the town treated us like celebrities."

It was a family affair—a father/daughter, sister/brother, and coach/player combination. A core of moms, who wore their daughters' numbers on T-shirts and screamed their heads off throughout every game before that was fashionable behavior, backed the players. My siblings, my grandpa, and I cheered for them every step of the way.

It was no coincidence that the first Illinois state championship tournament was held at the university where I played. The right people together at the right time made it happen. Illinois High School Association (IHSA) headquarters were located in Bloomington, and ISU was located in Normal, Bloomington's twin city.

Laura Mabry, ISU's Women's Athletic Director, and our coach Jill Hutchison (State Finals Manager) and the volleyball coach, Linda Herman (State Finals Assistant Manager) who later became an acclaimed athletic administrator, fought to host the event on their campus.

Even my teammates Cyndi Slayton, Kim Woodward, and Judy McNamara played a part as bench officials. Once again, relegated to the sideline, I assumed my role of spectator, cheerleader, and fan. Filled with bittersweet pride for my sisters, and a fleeting sense of regret, I once again felt the parade pass me by, but deep down I knew that without my pioneering role, they too would have been passed by.

I have always remembered the mom squad, my golden sisters, and the odd coaching trio, but never realized the efforts of Ola Bundy. Only after she passed away thirty years later was I even aware she existed. When my dad mailed her obituary to me, I acknowledged the loss of our unsung hero.[8] Without the First Lady of Girls' Interscholastic Athletics in Illinois fighting for our cause, women in the Land of Lincoln might have waited several more years before being given a chance to compete. During her 29-year career as an Illinois High School Association administrator, Ola Bundy led girls' athletics from GAA and intramurals into a full-scale 12-sport interscholastic tournament line-up, equivalent to the boys. With her feisty personality, she persuaded school administrators to allow girls' athletics a fair chance to develop. The majesty of the state tournament pageantry unfolding on my home college court was not lost on me.

In turn, my dad, who grew up emulating Coach Mac, later instilled those same values in the athletes he nurtured during his 33-year career at Sterling High School. His endearing relationship with his championship girls' team earned him the

---

[8] http://www.ihsa.org/announce/2005-06/060219.htm

affectionate title of Papa Mac. But he was always attributing the success to someone else.

"You started all this! Those girls wanted to be like you, the first Golden Girl," dad reminded me during the fanfare that followed, "but it's hard to be a pioneer."

He was only partially right. To this day, when I am back in my hometown, someone will recognize me and comment about my being "the girl who won a state championship." I used to smile and correct them, saying, "No, that was my baby sis, Karen." Now I just smile and nod. Over time my story and my little sister's became seamlessly intertwined; I no longer remember where one begins and the other one ends. Together we make up the rich tapestry of Sterling Warrior history in the Sauk Valley region in the Land of Lincoln.

If it couldn't be my dream to go to State,
Let it be my town's—Sterling.
If it wouldn't be my destiny to be the first player introduced,
Let it be my number—23.
If it wasn't to be my fortune to score the first basket and win the first game,
Let it be my name— McKinzie.
If it couldn't be part of the plan for me to become the first state champion,
Then let it be —
Part of my sister Karen's.

Chapter 5: College Ball Roadie

ISU, Normal Illinois 1977-1979

"You don't have to be a victim of your environment. You learn that through sports, you learn that through teamwork. You decide who you want to be and then you go pursue that."
Jill Hutchison [9]

I learned this key lesson from my college coach, a legend in women's basketball. She refused to be a victim of gender.

"Paul Bunyan, can you read me? Beavers' west I-74," Vonnie said into the CB radio. "What's the road like ahead?"

"Damn, get your ass off the road lil' Beavers!" The trucker yelled back. "It's a f****** blizzard here!"

As static drowned out the trucker's voice, the wind whipped across the plains so strongly that snow came down in horizontal sheets forming five-foot high drifts.

"Why aren't we stopping at a motel?" I asked.

"Sleep in the car. There's no money left in the budget," Vonnie said and then screamed, "Oh shit!" as our wagon spun out of control and fishtailed, heading straight at Coach's car that trailed us. Coach swerved and her car sailed into the median and stuck there. Everyone got out of the car to push, except Coach, who sat stuck in a snowdrift, drumming her fingers on the wheel. Vonnie tapped at the window. "Hey coach, should I give up the wheel and ride shotgun?"

"Vonnie, you're lucky I don't have a shotgun!"

In the fall of my junior year, I studied, but basketball was my real major. The season replaced holidays. We traveled to compete against Big Ten schools in a caravan of campus station wagons. In the days before cell phones, the cars maintained contact over CB radios and depended on truckers for updated weather reports and speed traps. After a few grueling all-day practices, we piled into cars for a New Year's tournament in Slippery Rock, Pennsylvania. I rode in the back end of the wagon, so I could rest my spine before and after games.

---

[9] *http://www.goredbirds.com/genrel/hutchison_jill00.html*

During the previous summer, I had twisted my lower back on a move and it hadn't been the same since. On road trips, Vonnie and I roomed together. Vonnie was short and solid as a rock. I was tall and wiry, though I filled out from weight training. Then after tournaments and conference games, we piled back in the wagons for the long ride back home. We were up for class the next morning and back in practice in the afternoon.

At the end of the semester, I had a 4.0 GPA and was averaging 20 points a game. Basketball remained my sole love. Coach, whom we addressed fondly as Hutch, told us to bulk up on carbohydrates before games, so Vonnie and I devoured pizza and donuts while drawing basketball plays on paper napkins.

Vonnie was a great ball handler and could pass on a dime. She had a sweet shot at the top of the key. If the 3-point shot had existed back then, she would have obliterated all scoring records. Char would set picks for me on the wing and, if the defense picked me up on the shot, I'd hit her as she rolled inside. Vonnie would nail me coming down the left side on a fast break. Together the seniors made me look good.

As first generation Title IX athletes, competitive sports for girls were so new that we came to college with little more than raw talent, true grit and a love of the game. Awed by Coach Hutchison, for the first time we had a female role model. Everyone who played for her wanted to do right by her.

"She would challenge us and only accept our best," said Olympian Charlotte Lewis, who kept one eye on the scoreboard and another on the bench. "If coach was standing up, we knew we weren't playing hard. If she was sitting down, we knew we were okay."

In retrospect, I never remember seeing Coach sit down in a practice or a game. However, she rarely rode the referees too hard even though at that time, she was the chair of the basketball rules committee.

One of the few times Coach received a technical foul was at James Madison University when she questioned the official's call. "I know I am right!" she shouted. "I wrote the rule!"

"Sit down, little lady," the referee yelled back, slapping her with the T anyway.

In the 1970s, like many large universities, ISU fielded three women's teams composed of thirty women. Back in the day before assistants, Hutch was a one-woman show. She planned practices, organized travel, recruited players, scouted opponents, and fought on national committees for women's rights. She mimeographed handwritten scouting reports detailing game strategy and opponent players' strengths and weaknesses.

Hutch had an uncanny ability to motivate players. Every game she scrawled individual notes to each player. "Pat you should have a blast tearing up Iowa's man-to-man defense."

I did.

Long before sport psychology existed, she invited a psychiatrist to teach us a progressive, relaxation technique before a game. I became so relaxed, I dozed off, but Vonnie giggled, setting off a chain reaction of team laughter. No way would psychobabble work with Von.

But it worked for me. I broke scoring records that year — with a broken finger. When I complained about a finger I'd jammed after deflecting a pass, I went to see Kathy Schniedwind, one of the first female athletic trainers, who later entered the Illinois Athletic Trainer's Hall of Fame. Like Hutch, Schnied was a pioneer.

Schnied sent me to Rachel Cooper Health Center where a doctor insinuated that I was a sissy, "Nothing, a little tape can't fix up, honey," he said. So with pain shooting from my pinky to my elbow, I adjusted my shot. Weeks later, Grandpa, who remained active as an assistant football coach and trainer at Eureka College, drove over to see our game. He took one look at my right hand and said, "Bet my last dollar that finger is busted — you need an X-ray."

I made an appointment with a specialist, who confirmed my grandpa's diagnosis, but explained that it was too late to fix the bone, which had already set. So to this day my fifth phalange sticks out like the broken arrow signpost indicating right turn allowed. Ironically, it remains the only pain free joint in my body.

During my junior year I lived in Dunn Barton Hall, the old four-story, red brick dormitory across from the women's old gym, where I worked out at all hours. I shot jumpers from the free throw line, the corner of the key, and the baseline. I started in close working the board shots then gradually moved out behind what later became the three-point line. I dribbled behind my back and between my legs, and then spun and shot.

After each rebound, I dribbled and set up for the next shot. Always on the move, I put up a hundred jump shots. Then I shot free throws to catch my breath before starting a new sequence. I worked my left hand twice as hard as my right, so that when I was in a game, I could drive and shoot a left-handed runner, hook, or stab shot.

McCormick Hall, known as the women's gym, was so old that my grandpa's teams from Eureka had played in it during the 1920s. It became my second home; the workout was my religion. Here, in the dimly lit half-flight gym, as the saggy wooden floor creaked, I transcended time. I could have been someone shooting from the turn of the 20th century or a century later. I pushed to better my time on stair runs and skipping rope. I was always shooting, working hard to hone the jumper, the free throw, and the drive and shoot on-the-run. Somewhere between one basket and the next, everyday problems dissolved into a perfect peace. The goal of being a great basketball player came second to this joy in movement. I bounced the ball in rhythm to Marvin Gaye, Grover Washington Jr. and Roy Ayers, but even without my jam box, the beat went on. A certain rhythm. A special song.

At times, that perfect melody came back to me in the heat of battle. I tuned out the opponents and fans, and turned into myself, flowing in that state of harmony where my body and the ball were as one, where every move was fluid, every shot a pure swish. My teammates, sensing the aura, set picks to get me open, while Vonnie fed me the ball. In the zone, my body took over the rhythm ingrained during long hours alone in the gym. In that perfect state, I broke the ISU scoring record—39 points in a game—and set a new single-game scoring record for the tournament.

In 1978, ISU hosted the AIAW Large School State Tournament. However, it was not in Horton where the men's team packed the 5,000-seat stadium; instead, we were relegated to University High gymnasium with a seating capacity of 200. We failed to fill the stands, but still put on a show. We beat Loyola 108-42, Western 103-72, and then upset first seed Northwestern in a semi-final. I knocked down 27 points and held archrival Mary Murphy to 12. Then we defeated third seed Southern Illinois University 66-62 to win the AIAW for the seventh consecutive time.

With Von feeding from the point, Charlotte and I became a

powerful one-two punch. After the game, I couldn't recall how I drove the baseline and reversed the ball up under the defense. Movement blurred. I only remembered Charlotte urging, "Shoot, Pat, shoot," as she screened off opponents with her muscular frame, giving me the split-second open look at the hoop. Sacrifice is part of any sport, but how does one explain that those with the fewest riches to offer, own the most generous souls? Big boned, plain-looking, poverty-stricken, Charlotte, whose only claim to fame was her gift for the game, helped set me up to break her individual game scoring record, as well as the record for most points scored in a state tournament.

None of us could understand the hardships Char endured growing up in Peoria's Taft Homes projects. She aggravated us by showing up late or failing to turn up for practice, but Coach would dismiss it and say "family problems," never revealing Char's difficulties. But each time Char was a no show, two petite, white women (Hutch and Schnied) drove to Peoria's inner-city to find Charlotte and bring her back to the fold.

No one doubted Char's tenacity to overcome all odds. She never played ball until college. She didn't graduate with her class in 1978. When her college eligibility ended, she went pro. After 15 years of professional ball abroad, Char returned to school. Hutch, never one to brag about her own accomplishments, was proudest of the fact that every athlete she coached in her 28-year tenure at ISU earned a college degree.

Back then our euphoria over an AIAW state victory was short-lived in the regional tournament at East Lansing Michigan. We got upset again, and lost our chance for a national title. After the defeat, I returned to the gym to train for the next season.

Months passed before I saw Phil again, but like old friends we picked up where we left off, as though no time had lapsed in between. Summers were bliss. I had a full-ride scholarship, so I could take an easy, low-wage summer job as a lifeguard. When I wasn't "working," I was in the gym. In the mornings, Phil and I played one-on-one and worked on new moves. In the afternoons, I worked and swam laps during my break. At night I returned to the gym for pick-up games with guys. Sometimes on my way home, my T-shirt and shorts bathed in sweat, I would stop off at Phil's, for a cold drink, Kool-Aid® or iced tea. Phil would be strumming the guitar or listening to music and I'd just hang around blending in with the furniture, watching the steady stream of visitors. Some nights after I'd been with friends, I'd swing by Phil's and holler through the back door, "Still up?"

"I wouldn't be if people didn't keep dropping in."

Then we would talk. I babbled about my problems or Phil would talk about teaching and I would listen, my eyes fixed on his own. Over summers, we shared all our thoughts and feelings and dreams.

My vow to never attempt to compete in international ball lasted less than a year, until the following spring; Vonnie and I stepped up our training program. In June we tried out for the Pan American team at St. Louis. Hundreds of girls were in the gym. The coaches gave us numbers to attach to our shirts, but in scrimmages we wore colored jerseys over our numbers.

"The only way you'll get the ball in a scrimmage," Vonnie said, "is to take the ball out and throw it in to yourself." For two days, we went through the motions of drills, aware that the coaches weren't watching us or anybody else. We left after the second day of tryouts when I got food poisoning from a fast food hamburger.

I had another shot at international ball through Athletes in Action, a religious organization that travels to European countries[10]. I filled out all the applications and they wrote back and said I'd been selected as an alternate for their team. I would train with the team in Boulder, Colorado, and if anyone got injured, I'd go on the tour. I went door to door, asking for donations to help pay for my flight and training camp. I felt ashamed to ask the community to invest in me, a maybe.

When I arrived in Boulder, the university was holding religious conventions. In the dining hall everyone bowed his or her head before taking a bite. Before we started the day, we took turns giving devotions. Before and after every practice, while the team prayed, "Watch over us and prevent injuries," I whispered, "Help me stop wishing someone gets hurt." These were the toughest two weeks of my life—helping build a team I would not be a part of. I was in great shape—the high altitude didn't bother me—but my conscience did.

---

[10] http://www.athletesinaction.org/

In the American competitive, capitalistic way, people there invested in gold crosses, leather Bibles and other flashy symbols. My own beliefs in God came into question. I grew up in the Methodist church—was baptized, partook of communion, the whole bit. But in high school, I fought the Sunday church ritual. I had yet to discover a church that was all-inclusive. I still believed in God, but questioned organized religion. At the end of the week, I remained confused, but one look at the Rockies kept my faith in God intact.

As soon as I returned to Sterling, I stormed into my basement room and flopped on my bed. I took my passport filled with blank pages for visas of places I'd never see, and flung it across the room. "Why did I waste money on this?"

"Don't throw it out yet. It's good for five years. You may need it someday," my mom said. "You're young. You can go wherever you want in your life. Have faith. Give Phil a call? He'll make you laugh again."

In July, Phil and I worked as counselors at the ISU summer basketball camp. Whatever motivation I lacked in my latest setback, he made up for. When the kids had a break, he shoved a leather ball in my hands, taunting, "C'mon, beat me just once." I drove, attacking the basket, propelling my body around or through Phil who always blocked the path to the hoop. I thought I hated him. When we stopped, I gasped for breath, holding back tears, realizing that the real opponent was myself.

My final year of college should have been a triumph, but instead I felt panic, as if time was running out. I was determined to get a teaching degree though I knew I would need to take an extra semester to finish.

The basketball season was equally frustrating. Vonnie, our talented point graduated, and Char, our Olympian center, finished eligibility, leaving me the lone returning starter and senior on a team with five freshmen during a building year. There was no time left for me.

Books, boys, bars, but my greatest diversion—basketball — became a free-for-all. In a pre-season scrimmage, an opponent went up for a rebound and landed on my back. I crawled to the sideline. A week later, when I still walked sideways, my roommates turned all the pictures in our townhouse sideways to cheer me up. An osteopath popped my back in place, but the pain remained. I returned to practice with a knife in my buttocks. I skipped classes because my leg went numb if I sat in a chair for long. I had to lie down before and after practice.

During the summer, Coach Hutchison was selected by the Amateur Basketball Association of the United States of America (ABAUSA) as head coach of the 1978 National Junior Olympic Team. Her work was cut out for her as she followed in the footsteps of legendary Pat Summitt, who coached the gold medal team in the Pan Am Confederation Junior Games. I knew my coach returned to the 1978-79 season with valuable experience and insight into the game, but no matter what strategy she tried in practice or games, we kept losing. As the season progressed, I felt the pressure mounting.

Over the Christmas break, the dorms closed, but we had basketball practice, so my team, which by now included Phil's sister Fran and my own sister Karen, who had transferred from Lacrosse, Wisconsin, camped out in my house. Confined to close quarters, we learned to accept our differences in age, background, and race. We, white girls slipped into a Black street slang and the Black players tolerated our bland, white folks' food. But our off-the-court cohesion never helped us on the court. We continued to lose games. Everyone enjoyed the road trips, except me. My back throbbed from riding in a car and my heart ached from the latest loss. Without my family's support, I could never have survived the season. Sue lived with us second semester and cooked me hot meals when I came home discouraged from another bad practice. Karen, now part of the team, patted my back in practice and whispered encouragement at half time. My parents and grandpa came to every home game and my dad still met me at the water fountain with advice.

The ISU basketball team had been a dynasty as one of the first powerhouses in women's basketball in the Midwest, but other teams caught up. My coach was obligated to juggle too many responsibilities without an assistant. She suffered, too, from loss but not as greatly. For a coach there is always next year. For a college student, the senior year marks the end of the season and very possibly the end of the road. Forever. No city leagues existed for women. A professional league started in 1978. Though three former teammates, Cindy, Vonnie and Char played in the league, they told me it was struggling to survive. Vonnie knew the score from her experience as an All Pro guard for Dayton Rockets in the 1978-79 season.

As the season dragged on, I forced myself to psych up for the game. I went through the routine, studied the plays, listened to music, and practiced the power of positive thinking. At the end of the game against Michigan State, I stared at the scoreboard in disbelief: one lousy point. At the restaurant with family, I slouched, picking at my fries.

"It's not your fault we lost," Karen said to console me.

"You had 29 points and 15 rebounds," Dad said. "Your team is inexperienced."

But we lost the following night to Memphis State, and the next weekend to Northern Kentucky. I bore the weight of the season on my shoulders; I felt that I had let the team down even though I had 18 points and 11 rebounds. The only stat the mattered to me was the win-loss percentage.

Not only was I an emotional wreck, my body was giving out. The constant ache in my lower back was tolerable, but every time I bent my knees, daggers seared the soft flesh under my kneecaps bringing tears to my eyes.

"Jumper's knee," the doctor diagnosed.

"White girls can't jump!" I said.

The doctor chuckled. "They also call it washerwoman's knee. Bursitis. Fluid builds up under the kneecap." He said, "You need to stay off the court."

"I can't! It's my last season."

"It'll get so painful you won't be able to walk. Ice them before and after games and take two of these a day."

"I don't want to take pain killers."

"Anti-inflammatory meds will help, but you'll still hurt."

I finished the season trying to keep the pain at bay with anti-inflammatory pills. Before and after games, I iced my knees, and then hobbled onto the court. At the jump circle, I bent my calf back to my thigh to loosen up my quads; my knee creaked like the Tin Man. Rest for a Division I athlete at the end of her career wasn't an option.

During every set back due to injury, my dad and Phil told me to study the game. Once in awhile, someone taped a game, but it was nothing like the videos of today. It was black and white reel to reel with a picture so grainy no one could distinguish offense from defense, let alone break down something as finely detailed as shooting form.

I couldn't sit still long enough to watch sports on TV or to attend men's games. I only wanted to play. I had Attention

Deficit Hyperactivity Disorder (ADHD) before the diagnosis even existed. My mom called me "scooter foot." As a kid, I sat at the table on one leg, the other foot on the floor ready to bolt, barely bothering to eat. I skipped, jogged, biked, and balanced on stilts, rather than *walk* to school.

But I had so many injuries my senior year that I would have been better off slowing down and red shirting. (The NCAA allows an injured athlete, usually a freshman, five years to complete four years of eligibility; the player continues to receive his or her scholarship, attend college and practice, but is not allowed to play in games.) But the concept may not have existed back then for women since scholarship money was so scarce. I never missed a game or practice, but I was driving my body into the ground.

From the time I turned 16, when the government finally allowed women on the court, basketball became an everyday passion. When my career as an ISU Redbird came to a screeching halt, my heart filled with impending doom.

On February 10th, 1979, ISU met up with our neighbor rival, the University of Illinois for my last home game in college. I arrived at Horton Field House early. In the empty men's locker room, I meditated in solitude. In the seventies, we carried "lockers" on our backs, in a bag stuffed with uniforms, ready to change in hallways, equipment rooms, and restrooms. During my senior year, we finally received new uniforms. In slow motion, I pulled on my short red shorts and white jersey with the red number 23. I perched a bare foot on the bench and meticulously padded the space between each crooked toe with foam to prevent blisters. Then I wrapped my sprained ankle in white athletic tape, pulled on my red striped, over-the-calf, tube socks and slipped on the thick red, kneepads. I laced my too-wide-for-my-skinny-feet men's basketball shoes with the trademark Adidas black stripes. Lastly, I pulled my dark, thick hair into a high Barbie doll ponytail. Then I reclined, flat on the bench and inhaled the sweaty, stuffy air imprinting a mental picture. Teammates filed in chattering in their usual pre-game banter, shattering the magic of the moment. No one sensed the difference. As the only senior on the team, everyone else had next year and the year after, for me this was it—the end of the line. When the official announced the starting lineup, my name echoed from the empty rafters. A handful of fans, parents, and friends, rose to stand in a cluster behind our bench as the team presented me with a homemade plaque, snapshots, slogans, and team memorabilia, lacquered to a varnished wooden board.

Only after the center jump did I forget the solemnity of the moment. Then the game became like any other battle, a desperate drive to win. I scored 26 points, was 12 for 13 from the field, but at the free throw line in the last 10 seconds, my perfect shot wavered and fell to the side of the rim. With three seconds left on the clock, Illinois' star freshman, Lisa Robinson, a girl I had tried to help Coach recruit for ISU, threw up a prayer and scored to win by one point, 67-68. As the horn sounded, the floor slid out from beneath me. I would go down in history as one of ISU's most prolific scorers, yet the image of my missed free throw senior night would haunt me for the rest of my life.

A few weeks later, we opened the single elimination tournament against Northern Illinois, a weaker team. Trying too hard to compensate for my young team's lack of experience, I picked up three fouls early in the game. In the second half, I hit seven straight baskets while the defense collapsed around me. Then the whistle blew, another foul, my fourth. I returned to the bench. With twelve minutes left in the game, Coach put me back in. I missed a jumper and crashed the boards. Another whistle. I fouled out. In four years of college basketball, I'd fouled out a total of three times. As I walked to the bench, opponents exploded into cheers of joy in anticipation of the great Illinois State University upset. In a backhanded tribute to my college career, I received my first standing ovation for losing the game. For seven straight years ISU had won the state championship. Our reign ended. So did my college career.

At the end of the bench, I fought tears, and cheered as the game slipped away. How ironic that NIU, where my grandpa coached my dad in the 1950s, was the college team that shamed me in the final days of my career.

"I'm sorry, especially for you," Hutch said. I squeezed her hand, unable to meet her eyes. I let her down. I'd had a successful career, but all I remembered were the losses, the failures.

I didn't see Coach again until late spring, when she called, "You free to go out for lunch and receive your Wade Trophy Finalist award?"

"Free lunch. Cool! But what's the Wade Trophy?"

"It's an award for the best basketball player in the United States. It's named after Margaret Wade, a famous coach who started the legendary girls' basketball program at Delta State."

After lunch, a hamburger and fries in the student union cafeteria, a representative from Personal Products presented me a plaque in a dingy, corner office. A photographer snapped a shot of a stranger shaking my hand making a mockery of my nomination as one of the top thirty female basketball players in the nation. I played for the love of the game, not for the fame. Yet, being presented the most prestigious award in a back room, an award sponsored by sanitary napkins, was demeaning, a shameful reminder that women don't count.

Male college athletes were treated like demi-gods; the girl jocks were labeled gay and considered social deviants. The football team never won games, yet the players paraded around campus boasting of new uniforms, new equipment, new cheerleaders. The guys on the men's basketball team devoured steak and flew to their away games; the women ate sandwiches and drove college station wagons to opponents' gyms. While a handful of family members cheered our exploits, thousands of fans exploded into applause as my male counterparts sprinted into the spotlight on the court in Horton Field House. I wondered what it felt like to be a man always in the limelight.

Nice girls finish last.

In the summer, I started down the long, lonely road to top fitness and a chance to play in the new pro league. Basketball—my constant—365 days a year. A blinding love for a silly game.

Without any local competition, I took up any challenge. When a football player wanted to play one-on-one, I went up for a rebound against a 220-pound defensive tackle and caught his shoulder in my rib. It hurt to breathe and when the pain didn't subside after days, I went in for X-rays. The doctor explained that the blow separated the rib from the cartilage that attaches to the sternum and assured me it would heal in time. I had no time. I returned to the gym, with a stabbing pain in my chest.

I played a pick-up game against some non-athletic guys who acted as though it were an NBA play-off. I saw a gap on the end line. As I drove the baseline, my defender, a step late, body checked me and knocked me flat. I heard my knee snap. I hobbled through the rest of the game, and when the others drank their icy beers, I iced my throbbing knee.

Since Phil and I started the first girls' basketball camp in the area, I coached at our local camp, but the pain in my knee got worse. I saw an orthopedic surgeon, who put me in a brace to stop the hemorrhaging under the fat pad.

The next week, I hobbled in the cast-like brace extending from my thigh to my calf, along the sideline beside Phil, encouraging girls at ISU's camp. Each counselor was assigned a team of high school campers to coach during games.

In my first real coaching gig, I wonder in retrospect, if Coach Hutchison hadn't fixed the tournament in my favor. She put Cathy Boswell on my team. Cathy led Joliet West High School to a state championship in 1978 and became an Illinois State All-American. She later became a member of Coach Pat Summitt's 1984 Olympic Gold Team[11].

So the only coaching I had to do was to make sure the ball got into Bos' hands. Good thing Cathy took over on the court because I was suspended in another dimension on the bench with pain so severe it clouded my judgment and blurred my perceptions.

At night I lay flat, humming spirituals and jiggling my legs, afraid I would be paralyzed if I fell asleep. Excruciating pain kept me awake.

In a daze the next day, I went through the motions of coaching, enduring the constant pain in my left knee while I wondered if my right leg existed. Phil rubbed Deep Heat® into my thigh and I couldn't feel the heat.

"Phil," I said, "pinch me."

"I just did!"

"I can't feel anything."

"You better see a doctor right away."

"Doctor! No!" I said. "He'll make me take time off."

"Other options? What do you want to do besides play?"

"I don't know."

"You can sort yourself out in the hospital."

"Hospital! Over my dead body."

---

[11] http://www.youtube.com/watch?v=deV42SspVOY

But sure enough, the next day the orthopedic doctor in Peoria tested my reflexes.

"Your knee will heal," the doctor said, "but I'm admitting you to the hospital immediately to save your leg!"

Chapter 6: Heartbreak Hotel

Peoria Illinois – Washington D.C. 1979

"It began in mid-July as an intriguing experiment, joining two outcasts in professional sports – Black owners and women players – in one venture called the Washington Metros."
Ken Denlinger, Washington Post November 4, 1979

In the summer of 1979, physical strength and femininity were non-compatible entities, female basketball players were oddities and "a league of their own" was considered downright insane. However, that summer after finishing college I got a call saying that I had been drafted into the Women's Basketball League (WBL), by a first-ever professional league expansion team, the Washington D.C. Metros. Drafted? I thought draft was a beer!

The euphoria was short-lived. For two weeks after the draft, I was locked in traction for my back in the St. Francis Hospital in Peoria. Traction became a playpen for my mind. Steel bars framed my bed. One bar was perpendicular at the foot and another at the head. A long horizontal bar extended the length of the bed. My calves, strapped in foam encasings secured with Velcro tabs attached to ropes, held 10-pound weights, which in theory, would relieve the pressure of the herniated disk between my fourth and fifth lumbar vertebrae.

One minute I was a mini-celebrity being recruited by the Chicago Hustle and Washington D.C. Metros, both clubs called me to express their interest, and being interviewed by the local radio and newspaper. Then in the next instant, I dropped into non-existence in a hospital in a city where I knew no one. Fate played a cruel joke. Was this the pay-off for hard work?

I could not turn; the muscles in my back, hips, and thighs ached from being pulled taut. Days became a blur of pain. When my sister Sue visited, I begged her to run water in the sink, to help me pee in a bedpan. Was this the same girl who willed herself to win ball games? Was this the perpetual motion girl, walking at nine months and never slowing down?

My ears perked up at the clatter of the cart that wheeled me from my prison to the therapy where my workout consisted of tightening my back muscles and pushing them to the table eight times. Highlights were calls and visits from family and friends. One day, Coach and Vonnie, a non-conformist artist, came to see me. Von had made me a framed photograph; an action shot of me in my Redbird uniform that was superimposed on a larger photograph of a basketball. I stared at the picture, speechless, with my legs strapped in place, the same legs that would've run into a brick wall for my coach.

A harried doctor explained that I'd reached a plateau. My right leg remained numb. He ordered a myelogram, where dye was injected into the spinal column for X-rays. My dad pumped every doctor who passed down the hall with the questions that I feared asking, "What kind of operation?" Mom, in her calm kindergarten teacher voice, recounted details in the outside world. When they left, I returned to my imaginary land of books until lights out, then reality slipped in with the night shadows. What if I couldn't play ball?

I awoke to the ring of the phone. "Ullo, dis is Francis, ze trainer for Asnières first division women team. We want you play in Paris? Yes?"

"What? I can't understand you."

"You play basket in France wiz us?"

My heart stopped. "I want to, but I have a back problem."

"What you say? You no problem? We pay you to go back. Back home. We pay plane, we pay flat, we pay car.... "

"No. It is my health."

"'Ealth? Sink about it. I call few days."

I hung up the phone and felt bewildered. He was talking about McKinzie, the star forward, not me, the invalid, who couldn't walk to the bathroom. This isn't Pat; it's her shadow. Wrong number. Pat's in the gym.

After the myelogram, my head pounded as if a bat cracked against my skull, the pain making me nauseous. I grasped Sue's arm and retched thick green bile.

"The bulging disk is pinching off nerves in your leg," the neurosurgeon said. "In the cases like this that I've seen, the patient always opted for surgery, but it is your decision."

I clenched the side of the bed and vomited. "Very few patients have a violent reaction. It'll be better tomorrow."

Tomorrow, Doc. Tomorrow, I'll be dead.

The phone interrupted my thoughts. The French basketball coach called inviting me to play in August, but it was already then mid-July. "Sorry I can't play. I'm having back trouble."

"Next year. You come next year," he said and hung up. Next year, felt like eternity as I pounded my fists into the bed.

Ten days later, the pain remained.

"Your prognosis is poor. Your leg gives out when you walk. You can't lift it an inch off the floor."

"Doc, you think I'll be able to play ball again?"

"Ball? I'd worry about walking again," the doctor said. "We'll let you go home. You can decide when you want to go ahead with surgery."

"What if I don't want surgery?"

"You may not have that choice."

On the excruciating ride home, I felt each bump. Yet when we stopped in a park for rest, God's spirit tickled my bare feet in the grass, in the sunshine warming my face, in the soft wind sweeping across my skin. When we drove up the driveway, Grandpa Mac, Grandma Olson, my maternal grandma, and Karen rushed out, hovering around me as if I were a wounded sparrow.

After weeks confined to my hospital room filled with whiteness, sickness, and death, I marveled at miles of rich Midwestern flatlands on my first walk. A golden butterfly fluttered between the corn stalks bursting from the black earth. Yet each step sent a spasm of pain down my butt, reminding me of the uncertainty of my future. Each time I put weight on my foot, my leg buckled. I should've been ecstatic to be walking again. Instead, the shadow of my past ran beside me, hopping, skipping, teasing as if to say, "Come run!"

Others always defined me as an athlete; I saw myself as an athlete, but I struggled to walk and couldn't begin to run. There are no crippled jocks.

"Phil, what if I'm not ready in time for training camp."

"Quit worrying about tomorrow. Put one foot in front of the other. Build up that leg muscle. It's weak from atrophy."

Phil's determination carried me where mine left off. After I left Phil's house, I drove to the outdoor court.

My hands trembled when I picked up my old basketball. Still me, McKinzie, the ponytailed weasel that loved to dip and glide, yet in someone else's body, reincarnated as a cripple. I couldn't feel if I was jumping; my leg had no sensation. I dragged my lame leg around the cement court.

Phil took me to a new doctor, a chiropractor. I'd spent my

lifetime in doctors' offices: orthodontist, dentist, dermatologist, osteopath, physical therapist, and orthopedic surgeon. The podiatrist insisted that if I didn't treat my crooked toes, I'd have back problems. Ditto for the orthodontist. Without proper bite alignment my spine would be crooked. Now a chiropractor swore he could cure everything from headaches to cramps to slipped disks, by manipulating the spine and relieving pressure on the nervous system. Initially, I was skeptical, but after five treatments, I believed. My leg grew stronger. The chiropractor showed me stretching and strengthening exercises and reiterated that I was responsible for my own health. I left his office with hope. The following day, the orthopedic surgeon in Peoria, shook his head in disbelief as he watched me walk without limping.

"You don't need surgery now—you may opt for it later. Never seen anybody recover from a herniated disk like this."

I never mentioned the divine intervention and my bone-cracking chiropractor. I trained as intensively as my body permitted. At the gym, I shot baskets for ten minutes and collapsed. Each day I increased my shooting workout by five minutes. Jumper's knee returned with the stabbing pain every time I bent my knee. The back of my right thigh and buttocks ached until my entire leg throbbed.

"Grab that loose ball," Phil yelled in workouts. "Rebound. Follow your shot." I moved like a robot, calculating how to get the ball with the least amount of pain. My offensive moves, once so natural, looked programmed. After our ball work out, I pulled springs for the upper body and lifted leg weights at Phil's, then swam endless laps at the country club. At sunset, I ran around the track, doing a mile, a 440-yard, and a 220-yard sprint. I dropped in the grass, watched the universe spinning above me as I gasped for breath and kneaded my aching right leg with a shaky hand.

In early August, I received my professional basketball contract with the Washington D.C. Metros. Seven thousand dollars for the eight-month season. I wanted to be a part of the first pro league even if it only covered living expenses. Contracts were supposed to be guarantees, but I knew there was no guarantee in this game or this body. When the official WBL papers arrived in the mail, I called a lawyer, signed a contract that guaranteed hard times, and flew to D.C. What did I, feminist Yankee, have in common with a former Black model and an inner city single mom? I was about to find out. As a rookie, 6'3" 180-pound teammates knocked me on my butt when I tried to drive the baseline.

Thirty girls gathered at Fort Belaval, a U.S. army base, where I looked up to my future teammates, Willodean "Dean" Harris, Charlene "Toy" McWhorter, and my roommate, Debbie Stewart. I was relieved when the coach had me shoot on the sideline.

The Blacks outnumbered the whites. Our business manager, secretary, and coach were Black. Except for a gray-tinted hairline and slight paunch, Nat Frazier, former Morgan State and New York Knick's coach, could pass for a young ball player.

"Don't be smokin' or drinkin' or goofin' off," he said tugging at the elastic waistband of his sweats. "I been successful in ever'thin' I do, specially basketball. I don't deal with no losers, y'all."

The sound of shoes screeching and players grunting as they clashed under the boards filled the gym with the familiar sounds of fierce competition. I had greater finesse shooting and driving to the hoop, but the women who were street-ball players were more physical and aggressive. My sheltered, middle-class life handicapped me on the court where only the toughest survived. No one would say, "Look out for the lil' white girl y'all, she's got a bad back."

I was friendly to all, yet wary of each. Within a day, segregation was evident. The Blacks in one van, whites in another, Blacks at one table, whites at another. The staff made a hero out of a returning veteran, a moody, Black guard built like a bulldozer, who called herself Sugar. Rather than uniting the group, she split us down the color line by refusing to talk to or pass the ball to whites.

Coach made cuts and sent everyone home for a week. He kept eighteen players for training camp. Then he'd choose a final twelve. As soon as I got back to Sterling, I went to the gym and Phil tried to prepare me for what lay ahead.

"Damn it, Pat, go for the ball," Phil shouted at me during our work out. "If you don't grab it, someone else will. Basketball is no longer a game; it's your bread and butter."

Instead of fighting harder, I froze, and felt like a teary-eyed schoolgirl. "React, Pat, move," Phil yelled. My fear of making a mistake left me immobilized. I had to make it, but what if?

Each day I waited for news telling me to report to camp, instead the coach called with postponements. Though grateful for the extra time to get in shape, I longed to get on with my life. Once the school year started, I felt like a child playing hooky. I could only play ball six or seven hours a day, and the rest of the time I was alone with my thoughts. Independence, that long-sought state, and its sidekick responsibility were mine. The mail brought doctors' bills and a car payment, making me an official member of the working world, but who would consider basketball a job for a girl? I tried to live one day at a time, in the moment, but whoever coined that term was never a single, unemployed 22-year-old, living at home in a small Midwestern town.

The phone rang at midnight; my coach told me that I would fly out at noon that day. Phil left work early to drive me to O'Hare airport in Chicago and with a hug nudged me away from home into the next adventure. After I landed in Washington D.C. airport, other players and I hung around the terminal until midnight waiting for the rest to fly in from across the U.S. Thus began my "hurry up to wait" group life.

The rookie camp had been so organized; we were surprised when the first practice of training camp was canceled because the coaches couldn't find a free gym. While waiting, I exchanged life stories with my new roommate, Cheese, a stocky 170-pound forward from the Bronx. I listened wide-eyed to her stories of gang fights and rapes in the inner city.

D.C. was a hustling city; survival depended on selling one's soul. The coach and managers, though friendly, were smooth-talking businessmen out to make a buck.

"Challenge the cutter," coach yelled. I stepped in front of our solid Black center when she rolled off a pick into the lane. My back cracked as it hit the hardwood after she forearmed me like a dummy in football practice.

"Shoot, McKinzie. You a shooting forward. Put the damn ball up," Coach screamed. As I released the ball, a hand slapped my arm and a hip nudged my thigh, knocking me off balance. I toppled backwards and the ball missed the rim.

"Air ball," my defender shouted, pumping her fist.

With each new practice, I discovered a new ache in my body. My lower back throbbed. Without anti-inflammatory drugs, I couldn't bend my knees. I could never make up for the lost time. The coach made or broke players. He yelled until I was immobilized with fear. Why was Mia, a walk on, playing my position? She couldn't shoot or drive!

My pride wouldn't let me quit. I had to win my spot. After being beaten up, I fell into bed. Did I hate the game because I was no longer the star? The struggle within me was greater than the turmoil between Blacks and whites, gays and straights, coach and players. This game was dirty and rough. Phil was right: "get the ball or starve." How could I fight my teammates? We were supposed to play together.

"McKinzie, get out," the coach yelled during a scrimmage. "You limpin' girl. Get out before y'all get hurt."

"I'm fine coach, I can play,"

"Don't be pushing it. I can keep you on taxi squad."

In the steam room, I collapsed against the wall; my hot, wet tears were lost in the moisture. Sidelined again.

Almost every day we changed roommates as players were cut, quit, or traded. One night the phone rang and my current roommate, a cute blonde guard, picked it up.

"No way!" she said, hung up and burst out laughing. "Coach wanted me to come give him a massage."

"Is he mad cause you said no?"

"Probably, but I'm not going to lay to play."

"He wouldn't do that," I said. "He's just a talker."

"Want to bet? Why do you think Mia plays? She wasn't drafted. She was a waitress. Miss "coffee, tea, or me" must be good in bed; she's in the starting line up."

We laughed that night, but we weren't laughing the next day when Coach gave my roommate a one-way ticket back West. Infuriated, I played strong at practice, but Coach saw my limp and pulled me. He insisted that the trainer take me to the chiropractor. My hip felt off balance. Pain shot down my right leg. My right calf cramped up, so I knew the sciatic nerve was being pinched.

"A curve in your lower back and neck acts as a shock absorber," the chiropractor said, "but you have no curvature in your neck, so your lower back has all the pressure on it."

"How soon can I play?" I asked, ignoring his warning.

On the ride back to the motel, the trainer suggested I consider the risk and speak to Coach. When I saw Coach, I was ready to give up the game I loved.

"McKinzie, one wrong move, y'all in a wheelchair. Y'all made the team. I'll put y'all on injured reserve."

I returned to rehab until the doctor released me. Then I went back to battle. Every move hurt. I no longer played with reckless abandon; I held back, afraid of being clobbered.

Too Tall, a gorgeous 6'4" former model, who averaged 20 points and 20 rebounds a game in college, was colorblind.

"Girl, I gotcha a sugar daddy," she said showing me a photograph of one of her many male suitors.

"Are you crazy? If your sisters see me with a brother, I'd be dead meat."

"Then, we goin' for a drink. C'mon girl. Just one."

She drove her Impala down Route 1 and parked at the country rock grease bar. We ordered a beer. The waitress returned with a pitcher and nodded at the bartender, who came to our table and asked for a date.

"Look like you got a lover," Too Tall said.

"He's too short."

"Oh, get out girl. They all the same size in bed," she said and threw her head back and laughed her deep, rich laugh.

"Where you white folk get all the hang ups? Everybody need it," she kidded, jostling me with her hand, like a spider, covering my shoulder.

The next morning, Coach moved me in with my rival Mia. We fought for the same position, yet got along well off the court. I wasn't surprised when Mia asked, "Girl, want to hang out with us."

In the beginning of November, Coach told us, "Y'all get dolled up today. The mayor of Washington D.C. wants to welcome us to the city."

Like schoolchildren in our Sunday best, we sat squirming in the lobby for two hours.

"Welcome to D.C., little ladies!" Mayor Barry said and shook our hands. Then he glanced at his watch and winked. "Excuse me, girls, I have urgent business waiting."

"We ain't ho's, we are athletes!" Dean said on our way out. Instead of feeling honored, we hung our heads in humiliation.

On the ride to our next game in Madison Square Garden, I sat by a girl nicknamed Sky because she was a white girl who could jump. She had the sweetest jump shot and a southern drawl. Since rookie camp we had hung out with different groups and, even though we were friends, I was surprised when she revealed her gay life.

"I had boyfriends. Then I became friends with another girl

and one night we kissed. It seemed wrong, but felt right. We fell in love."

I was afraid to blink or interrupt. The gays I'd known pretended to be straight. No one ever talked about it. I gazed into her green eyes, not wanting to offend her by looking away.

"I never envisioned kissing a girl," she said. "It was our first homosexual experience."

"What happened to her?"

"We split up. I was devastated. My college years were wild, until I started going with my Pam. In the summer, I met Callie and fell in love. I broke up with Pam and moved in with Callie. In the fall, we went back to separate colleges. Pam refused to speak to me; basketball was rough. When I moved to D.C. to play pro, Callie wanted to split up; I won't let her. I have $100 phone bills and write every day."

I looked at her anew. Gay love was painful, too.

"It's not like people think. I never meet girlfriends in gay bars. They promote the sex-starved stereotype of gays. I meet girls the same way you meet guys."

"What did your family say?"

"My grandma calls me deviant."

"Could you fall in love with a man?"

"I like men as friends, not as sex partners, but I can see a cute girl and feel turned on. I used to feel ashamed; now I think I have the best of both worlds, but it's hard to hide who you are. Ever been attracted to another woman?"

"I've liked you since rookie camp, but not sexually. You were sincere. At school, I was infatuated with a teacher; when I found out she was gay, I was turned off."

"Do I repulse you?" she asked. The pain of a lifetime flickered in her green eyes.

"Of course not. You are the first person who ever tried to explain what it was like, that ever gave me a chance to understand. It's my fault, too. If I knew a girl was gay, I avoided her, afraid of what people would think."

When we arrived in New York, people crowded the dirty, trash-laden streets surrounded by towering skyscrapers. In the restrooms, women in rags lay on the floor under newspapers. We warmed up in a barren 20,000-seat arena.

"Hey, where is everybody? This is The Garden!" our center, Toy, shouted at tip off.

Too Tall waved to the invisible crowd and whispered to me, "Girl, we like them bag ladies we seen outside. Nobody gives a hoot 'bout us neither."

When we returned from New York, players continued to hound the coach about being paid. For the last two months, we'd been promised paychecks and for the last three weeks he'd been saying we were moving into apartments.

"When are we moving to our apartments?" Sugar, our captain, demanded at our next team meeting.

"Real soon! I've got y'alls rooming assignments made up. They short on apartments, so we'll triple up."

We left his office and called the apartments and caught him in his lie. We returned to his office that afternoon.

"You lying Coach," Sugar said. "They got empty rooms. Guarantee us this three to a room stuff ain't gonna last all year."

"If y'all gonna fuss, I'll cut to ten players and the injured reserves will be in the street."

"No, we'll hang together," Sugar insisted.

I blinked back tears. Sky sensed my despair and asked if I wanted to go for a walk when we got back to the motel. We wandered to the edge of the woods and sat down by a tree. Unable to hide my shame any longer, I broke down. She patted my hand while I blurted out my fear of injury, and my frustration in sitting out waiting. "Better to wait than end up in hospital," Sky said while I pulled tufts of grass, peering at the trees, afraid someone would pop out and say "gotcha."

"What are you feeling?" she asked.

"Guilty," I said imagining the personal and social persecution gays must endure.

I went back to my room and tried to sleep, feeling confused about everything, especially sitting under a tree holding hands with a girl. I knew I was being judgmental. If it had been one of my straight female friends, it would be natural to comfort one another in a crisis.

So many times I wanted to call home, but I was scared that my folks would hear the self-doubt in my voice and I wanted to hide my despair. They already worried enough about my back. Instead, I called Phil collect.

"Hey Pat, how's it going?" Phil said.

"Bad! I'm at the chiros more than on the court."

"Everyone wants more playing time! You never knew what

it was like to go hungry," he said. "Your teammates do."

"Right Phil, I get it," I said. "Suck it up. Pro ball is not for sissies. But on this team everybody is going hungry."

The next day, we moved from the "Happy Inn" to the furnished apartments in Alexandria. Our complex, built to cater to the affluent singles, included a weight room and Jacuzzi. Yet when I shopped, I bought cheap staples — rice, potatoes, jelly — counting items at the checkout counter.

Like a farmer selling livestock to pay off debts, Coach kept sacrificing players. Too Tall was the next to go in a deal made with the St. Louis Streak.

We spent Monday in the Metros' office waiting for the coach to pay us and tell us where practice was. Three hours later, he sent us home; practice would be from 9 to 11 at night. Unpaid bills made it harder to find practice facilities. One day we even practiced on an outdoor tennis court.

The day before our opening game, we refused to play until we got paid. Finally we compromised and said we'd practice and play if we got paid after the game. We nicknamed the coach Daddy Digger, because of his nervous crotch-digging tic. When he talked to us he started scratching, and we knew "the man be lying again."

"I don feel like practicing," he said, his ego shattered by our doubt in his leadership.

We practiced on our own and for once we were a team.

Our first home game, a handful of fans saw us blown out of the gym by San Francisco. There's the future for the Metros. Everyday the papers published a new horror story. Ken Denlinger wrote in The Washington Post, "An agreement to play half of the home games in Baltimore ended in bitterness; most of the front office quit a month ago and the president of the league admits the Metros might be as much as $35,000 behind in paying those former employees and other bills."

We should have suspected something when the trainer, the general manager, and business manager walked.

"I've never been paid a dime," said Engelken, former vice president of operation/marketing. "I believe in women's basketball, but the Metros should have closed down and let us get on with our lives. I wasted a month."

"I'm giving them extra time," said Arthur Grant, the general manager of the Colony 7 Motel in Laurel. "You'll know how much they owe me if I sue. They stayed for a week in August."

The journalist's scoop confirmed our worst suspicions. Club ownership had changed three times. Rumors hinted at the team moving to another city or, worse yet, folding. After the game, the coach said he had to talk to some people and make some changes and I was sure that was my cue to being cut.

When we practiced in the Mt. Vernon college gym, half regulation size with cardboard backboards, I laughed at the absurdity of our pro life. We waited for hours in the Metro office for the coach to cash our paychecks. A week earlier, he had given each of us a check (mine was $326.48), but he told us that the banks wouldn't accept them; the club was having financial difficulties. He convinced us to endorse them so he could cash them. Trusting, naive, foolish women, we obeyed.

"Where's our money?" Sugar demanded.

"I feel terrible; I can't get your money," he grabbed his crotch with one hand and wiped his eye with the other.

The pretty executive secretary, who we suspected was the Coach's mistress, broke down sobbing, "I'm being evicted from my apartment, but I'm hanging on. I believe in Coach. He's doing everything he can; he loves y'all like family."

"Cut the crap," Sugar interrupted. "We'll hang, but get us a bird. It's Thanksgiving! We ain't had nothing hot to eat in weeks."

Digger bought groceries and my Black teammates cooked us a soul turkey, the best in my life. But practices continued to be sporadic. When Digger didn't show up for training, we played red light green light and ring-around-the-rosy for warm ups. The shakier our finances, the stronger our team bonded. When anyone got money from home, they invited the team for food and drinks.

After a scrimmage game against high school faculty, Digger offered to buy dinner: a bucket of chicken. We each got a piece of bird, a hard roll, and a glass of water. That night I fell asleep at 1:00 a.m. only to be wakened by the doorbell. Dean and Mia stood there, shell-shocked.

"Hey, my agent just called. We getting a 5'7" guard from Chicago," Dean said. "They be cutting somebody."

"Got anything to drink?" Mia said. She was scared too.

Every day I ran to get rid of my frustrations, then sat in a Jacuzzi and pretended I was rich. When I got home, I ate boiled potatoes and remembered I was po'. Why live in a luxurious singles' apartment when my cupboards were bare?

Our male coaches and managers tried to create a men's pro lifestyle on a women's league budget. We players knew that even "a little tit and lot of leg" would never sell—we couldn't put on the slam-dunking show of the big boys. We just wanted to play. We didn't need to ride in glass elevators, sleep on round beds in the Hyatt, and fly first-class on road trips. We didn't need a clubhouse, weight room, and Jacuzzi; we needed bread. But the highflying businessmen and former college and pro coaches wanted the NBA lifestyle in a ghetto league.

"We should sue their ass sky high," Dean said.

"Yeah," Mia said, "We need to call the newspapers!"

"The media couldn't give a damn about a bunch of dumb women who thought they could survive playing a silly game," I said. We worried about finances, yet waited for a miracle.

The next day at practice, I was so mad I shot every time I touched the ball, then I confronted him. "Rumor has it you're cutting some players, I should hear it from you."

"Why y'all think, you be going? Y'all a top draft pick."

"I know, but you hardly play me."

"Don't want y'all getting hurt, doll. League says I only carry 10 players; I ain't putting my girls in the street. We need a shooter. Get healthy, doll; I worry about the rest."

The next day, before the game, the coach announced that Duchess, one of my roommates, had been transferred to the California Dreams. We never even said good-bye. We drove to the Capitol Center and dressed for the game. From the bench, I watched us slip farther behind. He put me in and told me to "hustle!" With only 58 seconds left on the clock, there wasn't much I could do except hustle. Afterwards in the locker room, Coach yelled, "Our future depended on that game. Y'all blew it! All you had to do was win and we'd be 'live."

Then a representative from the league started talking, "We are looking for financial backers to take over, but if they don't, there'll be a dispersal draft. You ladies should know your coach has been working hard to make this succeed."

Daddy Digger stuck out his upper lip and began to cry. Our heads drooped in our hands. Players had given up solid paying jobs and used up lifetime savings for the "opportunity" to be a part of the women's first professional basketball league. Yet the Metros were 2—5 and we hadn't been paid for four months. After our game, I stayed to watch the Washington Bullets. Their victory in front of 20,000 frenzied fans accentuated our failure.

We boycotted practice the next day because no one had money for gas to get to the gym. Sky brought her leftovers to make a meal. My roommate cooked grits, Sky fried eggs and I made toast. After dinner, Mia and Dean called and wanted me to hang with them so I left.

After the following practice, Mia, Dean and I drove over to the Hyatt Regency to see the Atlantic Hawks, who were in town to play the Bullets. ,

"Better quit hanging with Sky," Mia teased, "She'll try to convert y'all."

I shuddered silently feeling ashamed for lacking the courage to confront Mia in defense of my gay friends. Why couldn't we all get along? After all, we were teammates. People still ignorantly assumed homosexuality was like cooties, something that could rub off on you if you got too close.

Mia was from Atlanta and had a "homeboy" on the team, Tree Rollins. They were in town for a game against the Bullets and invited us over to their room. When Tree opened the door, my mouth fell open. At 7'3" and 290 pounds he sprawled out diagonally across a king size bed, his thick brown legs sticking out of his shorts like tree trunks. Adidas, size 19, like barges, blocked the bathroom door. I was in a modern-day Paul Bunyan museum. Mia went into her number, brushing her body against him. As if we were some kind of freak circus sideshow, he was curious about the WBL. When we told him the top salary was only ten grand, except for marquee players like Ann Meyers, he rolled off the bed laughing.

"What about benefits? Retirement? Per diem?"

"What you be talking 'bout, boy? We ain't got nothing," Dean said, "even our Blue Cross, Blue Shield folded."

Tree saw the hunger in our eyes and ordered room service to bring up sandwiches, which we devoured. Then Dean said, "Let's hit it." Tree promised Mia gifts if she'd stay. He wrote off everything, even our parking ticket. He gave us a hug. Even Dean looked like a toddler next to him.

"Mia, why did you leave him?" Dean said. "You got you a big time sugar daddy."

"Oh, get out girl, he'd rip me in two."

We finally won a home game, so we were pumped at practice and happy at the prospect of finally being paid. As usual, Coach arrived "a day late and a dolla short." Next practice he never showed up; we worked out on our own. Determined, dedicated, dumb women. Exploited by sheer desire to succeed.

The next morning another teammate moved into our apartment because Daddy officially threw her in the streets. Coach called another emergency meeting at his office and while we waited Sky read the newspaper.

"Hey, listen to this. We made the Washington Post," she said, reading aloud.

It was three minutes until game time and Capital Centre, that red, white and blue monument to sports capitalism, was empty. There were perhaps 100 people in the building, including the players and coaches of the Metros and their opponents, the New Jersey Gems.

"They tell you, you're the pioneers," said Donna Geils of New Jersey Gems. "They know how great their desire is to play," she continues referring to the Metros, "And, in a way, their desire to play is being exploited."

Carmen "Cheese" Fletcher was asked if she felt exploited, "Without a doubt. Maybe a man feels like whenever he gets women together in a group or a team, that makes him a pimp and he can do with them as they please."

The Metro coach said, "If they are being exploited, I'm being exploited too."

"They got us by da balls," Dean said and we laughed.

Three hours later, Daddy showed up with more stories.

"The league has promised to pay ya'll next Thursday. If they don't, that's it. We can't go on," Daddy Digger said. His sad brown eyes drooped to half-mast, like a sleepy puppy, when he started in about how much money he lost and how his kids would starve. "I been going rounds with the league."

"We heard that shit before," Sugar interrupted, "Where's our money?"

"We are $55,000 in debt ladies, but we not the only team having financial difficulties. Now I jus' discover I am the highest paid coach in the league, which I wasn't aware of b'fore. I'm willing to give it to y'all."

"You mean you been getting paid?" Sugar was livid.

"Not really. Ever' penny I made I invested in this club. I am a sponsor, not just coach. The league goin' try to move us cause we got no support here. We movin' to Cleveland or

Baltimore, if they find new owners. We'll fly to Houston for games. Reserves stay home. Sorry, there's no money."

We didn't argue, didn't protest; we had lost our fight long ago. We had nothing else to go on, so we hung by his words even though we knew he was a damn liar. We'd come too far, worked too hard, suffered too much and waited too long to let go. We'd hang.

"Need some paper, girl?" Dean asked, offering me some money when the team left reserves behind.

"I'll be all right," I said, touched at her offer.

"Y'all got enough for the weekend?" Sugar asked.

"I can hang," I said, amazed at their generosity.

"We can give y'all what is left in our fridge. It'll just rot while we be gone," Dean offered. "Besides, Cheese is living with y'all and that girl can eat."

I'd been on a liquid diet. With my last $5, I bought bread, milk, and eggs. When anyone received money from home, they bought beer and pretzels and threw a party. Stuck on the poverty wheel, too broke to save, we blew our money. However, the greater the financial straits, the tighter we grew.

I hung out with gay teammates so often I no longer noticed any difference. They never pressured me into their lifestyle, yet I feared what other teammates would think. I began to understand their oppression and alienation. Ironically, our new trade, a pretty, blonde guard, who was the league's darling, was a lesbian. In trying to market our game, the media promoted her like a Barbie, advertising her as a sexual object. Wouldn't the public be astounded if they knew the sexiest player was gay? Who would come watch our games then?

The pressure of survival made everyone anxious. Coach was thrown out of games for swearing at the refs. Dean's agent said the team was going under. Newspapers stated that a new coach had been hired and different investors were looking at the team. We, the team, knew nothing.

The next morning, Dean rang the doorbell and woke me. Her agent heard the team was folding; she came to say good-bye before she flew home.

"Damn," I muttered. "Dean can't hang?"

You only hang so long. We were strangling by our own rope, our lifeline — basketball. We sat by phones waiting for a call to tell us where to practice, but practices were canceled. We waited hours in the office for a paycheck, but when we got it, the paycheck bounced or the bank it was written from closed. Suckers. We swallowed it all, praying that somehow it would work out.

Throughout the entire ordeal, I rarely spoke to my family. Without any income coming in, long distance phone calls were out of the question. I could call home collect, but I was afraid that if I heard my parents' voices, I would break down. I wanted to protect them from knowing how horrible the situation really was. Ironically, my folks had heard on the CBS news that our team had folded. The public in Illinois knew before the team players in D.C. We were the last to realize we were being screwed. Ah, the glorious life of a pro!

I only remember the anguish of injury and spending my savings for chiropractic adjustments, so I could keep playing. I recall sitting in an office filled with hungry teammates waiting for a paycheck that never materialized and lowering my eyes when we begged for gas money to get to the gym where we practiced by ourselves. Coach, seeing the writing on the wall, became a no show.

I can still hear the ball rebound off the hardwood and echo from the rafters in an empty Madison Square Garden, the Mecca of basketball.

I can still hear the concierge's voice when she waved an eviction notice under my nose and threatened, "Squatters! Get out of my apartment by tomorrow or I'm calling the police. Hear me, I said T-O-M-O-R-R-O-W!"

I can still taste Too Tall's cooking; her black magic could turn a piece of bird, pot of rice, and handful of pepper into a feast. When she was traded to St. Louis so quickly, we never had time to say goodbye. My roommate, Accronetta "Neat" Cooper, lamented, "We'll never survive. Your potatoes taste like paste."

I can still feel my head, like a fifty-pound stone, drop in my hands in the locker room when we lost the big one and hadn't been paid for four months. I've forgotten the coarse words of my angry coach, but I will always remember hearing the soft sobs of my toughest teammate, Bertha Hardy, wailing about her starving baby back home. To this day, I can still hear the hungry cry of her daughter echo from my own womb.

I witnessed a grown man break down for the first time when my coach and part owner, blubbered, "I lost my life's savings, mortgaged my $80,000 house, can't pay for..."

What next, God? For months, I wiped my feet on goodwill and hung by my faith and now what? We lived a modified hell. We weren't starving, but we were hungry. We weren't in the street, but we lived a day-to-day street life and made confetti out of our eviction notices. My phone rang nonstop with a player-to-player hotline.

"What's goin' down?"

"F—-if I know, ask yo' daddy."

And where was our damn daddy? On his knees in tears. He'd lost everything, his home, his savings, and his pride. He told us to meet at Sugar's apartment. Players filed in one by one without the usual banter. No one felt like laughing, no one talked. If we could have, we would have hugged and hung on physically, the way we'd held on emotionally for months. We couldn't cry; our tears had hardened into stone. We couldn't hug; we'd already touched one another too deeply. We had to forget we were friends and leave each other's lives the way we entered—as perfect strangers. We exchanged addresses. Someone suggested we plan a reunion, but we knew we wouldn't keep in contact. We couldn't. We shared only the time we were Metros. For that time, like family, we grew together, bonded by our common love for basketball. When the bond dissolved, we had to go our own way without looking back because "we" were no more. D.C., a city of politicians, was where everybody talked a good game, but with so much bullshit going on, nobody could distinguish the trash from the truth.

Sky, first to leave, hugged me. "I'll miss y'all."

"Me too." I wanted to thank her for sharing her world. Because I learned to love her the way she was, I developed an appreciation for the once-taboo, misunderstood homosexuals. Homophobia was as contemptible as racism, sexism or any other intolerance.

Phone calls flooded Sugar's apartment. Coaches from other teams called picking up players. Teammates stared at each other waiting to see who would get called next. When St. Louis called me, my adrenaline kicked in and my heart skipped a beat.

Later that afternoon, we met back at Sugar's when Coach finally showed up. Everyone bubbled with excitement about where they were going. Sugar to Milwaukee, Deb and Sky to Dallas, Dean to Iowa, Lou to Frisco, me to St. Louis.

Daddy called us into the bedroom one at a time. I thought I'd tell him off, but when I saw his sad brown eyes, and downtrodden form slumped in a chair, I felt pity.

"I was just getting ready to trade a player and put you on active. Should of done it earlier, but y'all got to believe me, baby, I worried about y'all getting hurt. Someday y'all be grateful I made you wait." Then he continued, "St. Louis picked y'all cause you a high draft choice. Don't tell them 'bout your back. It gets to be a psychological thing if a coach has to worry about a player bein' paralyzed."

I just stared at him in disbelief. "Now I'm gonna tell you the same thing I tol' the other girls. I love y'all like family. Soon as I get backers, I'm puttin' this team back togetha. We'll play in Baltimore and take it all."

"Sure, Coach," I mused, "like you'll pay us on Friday."

"Now c'mon give me some sugar, doll," he said. Dutifully I stepped forward into his embrace. Then my stiff form melted.

I hoped history would look back kindly on this broken man who dared to believe in women. It started with high hopes joining two outcasts — it ended in disaster.

We were both victims of our dreams in a society that refused to let us fulfill them because of its biases and preconceived notions.

We never gave up, but our team did and filed for bankruptcy. On Christmas Eve 1979, we split up in despair over broken promises and dashed hopes. Unknowingly, each of us left D.C. a lot stronger for having been a part of this rag-tag group of women who dared to sacrifice their souls to become one team, one dream — even for one season.

Chapter 7: A Dream Dissolves

St. Louis, Missouri, winter 1980

Bill Byrnes' brainchild, the first ever women's professional basketball league, lasted three years 1978-1981. Nearly two decades later, on June 21, 1996, a new dream takes flight, the inaugural WNBA season begins.

I walked into the house at dawn, after sixteen straight hours on the road. I stuck a note on the table, "look what Santa left," then curled up under the Christmas tree wrapped up in Gram's afghan just like I used to do as a child. I fell asleep dreaming of candy canes, sugar cookies, and evergreen. Why couldn't Santa be real and little girls remain innocent?

On Christmas Day, I headed to the gym. When I spotted Phil, I ran and wrapped him in a bear hug. He grinned, but once we started the game, his demeanor changed. Phil held the ball past the free throw line and then drove to the hoop. As I bent down in my defensive stance and lunged to stop him, a sharp pain ripped through my lower back. I limped off the court unable to move laterally. My chiropractor met me at his office. "No ball for two weeks!"

But the St. Louis coach, Larry Gillmore, called and told me I needed to report to practice in twenty-four hours. I put off making my decision about whether to show up for another shaky team, but I knew there was no decision to be made. Dad and Grandpa's silent applause, entangled with love, was etched across their faces in the pride filling their eyes. I didn't want to disappoint them. If the President was still in awe of my grandpa, imagine the reverence I felt for the grandfather whose work ethic and high morals influenced every step of my life.

"My respect for Mac as a coach and as a person is unlimited," Ronald Reagan said. "I still call him "sir" and I still mean it."

My grandpa could fill a small museum with trophies from championship teams. He dismissed those. Grandpa's greatest reward was seeing the kind of men his players became.

During a low point in his personal career, Reagan wrote my grandpa, "A coach's real record is how well the men who played for him can dig in when, in later life, the breaks are sometimes bad and the going tough. On that basis, Mac, your years are all in the win column."

I wanted to be a winner, too. So I ignored the doctor's recommendation and hit the road, feeling as if I were driving a matchbox car on a giant game board.

In St. Louis, I met the general manager and owner, Vince Gennaro, who talked about players in statistics, as if they were livestock, with a dollar value reflected in the baskets scored. I moved in with five girls and slept in the living room on a cot for the players who were traded or cut. I rode with them to the game at Keil Auditorium in a rough neighborhood, like the D.C. Armory where we'd had some games. Too Tall, already a part of the Streak team, walked into the locker-room, gave me a hug, and started babbling. The players kidded. Then suddenly, everyone stopped and froze, except Too Tall.

"God damn it, Too Tall," a medium-built man with a receding hairline swore. "I tell you to be ready at 7 o'clock, I mean 7 o'clock, not seven-o-five. You talk too much. Your mouth always gets you in trouble. You owe me $50."

The players stared at the white man who breathed fire, afraid to look away for a second. "Iowa is tough. You won the last six games, so you think you're King Shit. Know what I think? I think your head's too f***ing big. Iowa's gonna blow your ass off the court." He shouted and clenched his fists. "Go get 'em! You embarrass me, and I'll send you home crying."

My first impulse was to bolt. Instead, I sat on the bench and wondered what I was doing there. Guillotine, as we called him, verbally chopped off players' heads, and not just his own players' heads. He yelled at opponents, refs, fans, and scorekeepers as he paced the sideline. His language could shock players in a National Football League (NFL) locker room. Nothing had prepared me for this kind of abuse.

The next morning, my stomach churned. I was afraid to practice and get hurt, but I was more terrified of sitting out and receiving Guillotine's wrath. The coach taught the new players the plays. I did fine until he made me play defense. Every time, I bent my knees, sliding into defensive position, a knife in my back stopped my movement.

"McKinzie, quit loafing," he yelled. "Stay low. Step in front of the cutter."

I couldn't bend over to cover a girl crashing the lane, so I faked my way through practice, infuriating Guillotine.

"Damn it, McKinzie! You move like an old lady."

"F-you," my heart screamed back silently. I wasn't a person; I was an object, a commodity.

After practice Guillotine told five of us that we weren't traveling. "Might take you next trip, might pay you on a game basis or might tell you to go to hell," he said and laughed. But none of us believed he was joking.

I called home. "Finances are shaky. I'm hanging it up."

"You sure?" my dad asked. "You worked so hard. I'll finance you if you want to give it a try."

"No, Dad, I can't accept that."

"Look, it'd be like graduate school."

"No, " I thought. "Can't you see I want out? This is my out. Broke. Flat busted. End of the line." But instead I whispered, "Okay, I'll give it another week." I could let myself down, but I could never disappoint Dad, my life long coach, who had always supported my dreams.

I sat in Mickey D's (McDonald's®) eating my one-a-day meal, a greasy quarter pounder. I was used to walking into places alone, eating alone, shopping alone, running alone, sleeping alone. I could cope with the loneliness of the physical functions of everyday life, but I couldn't bear the mental anguish alone.

At home people believed the WBL lifestyle, like the NBA, was glamorous. They had no clue that going pro meant going to bed hungry and waking up to eviction notices. I no longer had to cling to that pioneer, golden girl identity. My experience in the pros left me jaded and disillusioned with the game. At the end of each season, we were has-beens. Trophies tarnish to make way for younger heroes setting new records next year. Could I live with myself if I quit the game I loved? Every day I packed my bags, in my mind, begging to have the guts to walk away. Players threatened to leave, but we remained locked in place, prisoners of our dreams.

I made new friends, but grew weary from the pettiness: the back-stabbing, bad-mouthing, catty things women did to each other, whether it be competition over a man or for a position on a team. Confined, we had no outlets or interests other than basketball and each other's business. The women spent their free time playing cards, watching soaps and bitching—all three of which bored me.

Players on the St. Louis Streak, like the Washington Metros, were exploited. Blabby, a 27-year-old, outspoken, business-minded woman told us how the club ripped us off. "You know what the turnover rate is in this club? Some days I make four trips to the airport to pick up new players and drop off the old. I've had twelve roommates."

The rumors in the league were so far-fetched that even as we lived out the drama, we had a hard time believing it.

"Imagine going to a strange city and trying out for the team, and being dropped off on someone's doorstep?" Ann Platte said. "We weren't making money and they weren't making money. We had to feed and house them like a Motel 6."

Players in the league rarely remained with the same club. Line-ups changed weekly, but nowhere as fast as St. Louis. Arriving here was like stepping into a revolving door. Gillman exchanged players so often other coaches called him Trader Vic. "Gillman is a regular Dutch scrubber," the St. Louis Post-Dispatcher reported. "When he cleans house, he cleans house."

"You getting paid?" I asked my new teammates.

"Paid? If you could call it that," Blabby said. "I demanded health insurance—the club has none—so they deduct the coverage from my check. They reimbursed gas for airport runs, and then took it out of the next check. Told me it was a down payment on my apartment. We need to confront the coach as a group, but Captain says it'll jeopardize too many players."

"Everybody's getting paid?"

"Not regularly. Newcomers haven't been paid at all."

"They keep saying they'll draw a contract," I said. "I came from a team that folded; I'm lucky teammates give me food."

"Fefe's worse off then you," Too Tall interrupted. "They been doggin' her. They cut her, then called her back. She quit a $7 an hour job. Now they got new players and want her to go."

"When I came, they gave me $400 in cash," said a player traded from the Chicago Hustle. "That was a month ago and I still haven't been paid. I never got my last paycheck in Chicago either, even though we drew crowds."

"Where's Connie?" I asked. "I haven't seen her since the first day."

"Oh girl, she is smart. Flew home after her first practice,"

Too Tall said. "A waste. A draft pick. Players come and go all in the same day 'cause a Guillotine."

The players only defense in the league was the grapevine of gossip between teams. Vonnie, my college teammate, warned me, "Watch out for Guillotine. He's a bastard."

"That man, never happy unless he makin' everybody else miserable," Too Tall said stretching her long legs across everyone else on the couch.

"He's an egotistical, high strung, foul-mouthed fool," one starter said. "He yells stuff I wouldn't say to a dog."

"Tell her about da day he threw ya out of the gym."

"He screamed at me so much in practice, I threw the ball away on purpose. "What kind of pass was that?" He yelled, so I screamed back, "A bad one." He told me to take the day off, I said, "y'all so sweet," in my southern drawl. Then he shouted, "Take two days off, smart-assed bitch," so I shut up."

"Tell 'em your story, Liz."

"He yelled at me everyday in practice. One day he even took a swing at me and I ducked. He suspended me; I went home. Then they talked me into coming back."

"Coach will tell y'all she begged to come back," said another player. "You showed him. Scored 25 in your first game back. Our Liz the Whiz leads the league in scoring."

"To this day, I wish I'd never ducked, then I coulda slugged him back," said Liz Silcott, the 5'6" Canadian guard, who was the league's best and most controversial player.

Every day someone was on the verge of quitting. We were traded like marbles. We never knew where we'd be tomorrow. We played with empty pockets, in empty stadiums for the same reason we played in the streets as kids. Glib businessmen and hardened coaches exploited our desire, trying to make a buck humiliating women. Women, in a man's world, struggled to make it in the big boys' game.

"We drew big crowds, but still had financial trouble," said another new trade. "Milwaukee players haven't been paid either. When it comes right down to it, it's nothing more than slavery. C'mon, our name is "Does," and our logo is a white tailed, deer that looks like a Playboy bunny!"

I was 135-pounds of prime rib for sale to be bought and branded in the WBL meat market.

I vowed I'd leave, but I'd wait until after practice. One last shot. In the gym I picked up a ball and knocked down jumpers with that wonderful I-don't-give-a-shit feeling. Nothing Guillotine could say would bother me. I took my shot, drove to the hoop and played with extra intensity. Midway through practice somewhere between sinking a 25-footer and sliding across the baseline, I realized I couldn't quit yet. They needed a shooting forward. After practice, teammates told me I looked good, but I didn't feel good. My right leg ached even during the warm-up and by the end of practice my back throbbed. At night spasms in my right leg kept me awake. Too Tall wanted me to go watch a guys' game. Then she bought dinner, pressed $10 into my hand and hugged me goodnight.

The next day at practice Guillotine played me for two minutes, just long enough for me to throw the ball away. After practice he told us he was taking the same people on the trip. When players walked into the locker room I asked, "You need me? If not, I'm wasting my time. I'm broke. I need a job."

"We need a pure shooter, but your weak side defense sucks! You move like you got a steel rod up your ass," Guillotine said. "Hang around, we'll find some cash."

Damn him. He knew I wanted to play. I couldn't take never knowing what team I'd be on or if I'd even have a team or thinking that I'd get hit and never get up again. I was tired of trying to prove myself, of falling asleep at night with one eye open and getting up in the morning with only one foot on the ground. Every night I dreamed I told off the coach and quit, as if my unconscious mind were deciding for me.

To escape, the women went out to a disco, swinging their hips, selling their souls for one-night stands. I was lost and directionless, trying to decide by not deciding.

I sat around all day with nothing to do, dependent on an organization I didn't even belong to. I waited five months in good faith to be paid for a job I was never given the chance to perform. "Either I get paid tomorrow or I leave," I told the manager. They wanted to keep me, but on their own terms. If a player got hurt, I'd be another dummy on defense. For the first time in my life, I prayed for the courage to give up.

In retrospect, we were ahead of our time, destined to fail. Racism, chauvinism, and sexism were deeply ingrained, especially in the macho world of basketball. Even the clever businessman and successful NBA coaches couldn't save us, but they tried. California Dreams owner, Larry Kozlicki, required players to attend classes at John Robert Powers' Charm School to increase marketability. The carefully chosen club names of Chicago Hustle, Minnesota Fillies and Milwaukee Does played into the sales pitch of femininity and sex appeal. Premier players that were highlighted for marketing value included Molly Bolin in Iowa, who never played the 5-on-5 game version, Janie Fincher in Chicago, and Faye and Kay Young, the Dannon® Yogurt twins in New York. Though topnotch players, they became star features in the WBL for meeting major criteria — white and blonde — that had nothing to do with their athleticism and everything to do with marketing. Cute, golden guards became the media darlings instead of the powerful African American centers like my teammates Toy or Dean or Char with their sculptured biceps.

The only thing that made any club newsworthy was scandal, like when a club declared bankruptcy. Or when the Chicago Hustle Coach Doug Bruno started a brawl by attacking the referee during a heated Chicago vs. St. Louis battle. Or when Nebraska Wranglers player, Connie Kunzman, was murdered.

Some teammates went to other clubs, some turned to coaching, some to men and marriage, and others flew abroad to continue playing.

In February of 1980, I left St. Louis on a well-planned whim. The league was in dire straits, but would hobble along for another season until it folded in 1981. I bowed out early. After another sleepless night, I packed and left. No good-byes. No second thoughts. I didn't notify the general manager to see if I would be paid; I was afraid if he gave me a check I'd stay. A teammate was sick and I might play, but I was tired of "maybe." I left, retaining the luxury of wondering whether if maybe I had endured longer, I would have made it. I didn't get cut; I quit.

As soon as I left the apartment, I drove to Port Plaza and walked into a beauty shop. "Do whatever you want," I said and closed my eyes. I no longer needed to defend the image of a straight, feminine, longhaired jock. Four hours later, I left with my hair in a short tight perm and an $88 Master Charge bill. I had barely driven out of town when I started fantasizing about playing ball... What about in Venezuela? Where the heck is Venezuela?

Chapter 8: Fast Break

Illinois, spring 1980

Home is where you lay your head.

In my adolescent fantasies, I envisioned challenging street ball players across the USA to one-on-one duels, loser buys dinner. After my college eligibility expired, I came close to doing just that, but it wasn't as much fun as I had dreamed it would be. Within the span of nine months, I lived in a townhouse cellar in Normal, a hospital in Peoria, in a motel on Route 1 Virginia, and a single's apartment in Alexandria. I crashed for weeks on the floor in a teammate's place in St. Louis and slept at a boyfriend's sister's home in Washington D.C., but by far my worst living arrangement was the backroom of the creepy, former funeral parlor in Peoria. Back in the 1920s during Peoria's exciting vaudeville days, this rambling Victorian mansion served as a brothel catering to showboats cruising the Mississippi River and visitors taking in the city's burlesque.

After I left the St. Louis Streak, I moved back East to Alexandria and worked round the clock as a substitute teacher by day, and cocktail waitress by night, trying to pay off bills incurred during my brief stint in the ghetto of women's professional basketball. In the spring, I drove back to Illinois to finish student-teaching at East Peoria High School. Too proud to borrow more money from my parents or grandpa, I rented a room in the dilapidated manor on the main thoroughfare leading to downtown Peoria.

During their teaching careers, my grandparents provided free room and board to needy college students to help defer the costs of education. My grandpa, son of a tenet farmer, defied the odds not only by earning a university degree, but also by providing the means for dozens of other poor men to pursue their dream through athletics and education. Grandpa and Grandma McKinzie lived frugally, only to spend their money on their grandchildren. Their financial support helped all four of us afford college, including Cornell, an Ivy League school, for my Merit Scholar big brother. Without batting an eyelid, Grandpa would hand me a check, another one of the magic loans that never drew interest and was more often than not a gift in disguise, for the only payback he ever expected was a phone call now and then. Yet it was also my stubborn pride, another trait I inherited from him, which made me reluctant to ask for help.

As a student teacher at East Peoria High, I spent lunch hours at my desk, where I retrieved lunch from my backpack. I nibbled a peanut butter and jelly sandwich that tasted like tennis shoes, sipped an 8-cent carton of milk and scribbled stories in a torn notebook, wondering what I was doing here. Coaching track was the best part of being a teacher. At track meets, I chased my distance runners around the track, dashing to the corner to shout their split times and then racing back to the finish to catch them as they collapsed at the end line.

On a weekend home from student-teaching, I saw Phil again and I was furious, not at him, but for him. He resigned from coaching the boys' basketball team because they were hiring somebody outside the district as head coach, even though he'd been working with the team for ten years.

"The ones they are hurting most have nothing to do with it—you and the kids."

"I've been trying to tell you, it's a black and white world. This community thinks it's above prejudice. I'd rather have someone tell me to my face they didn't like the color of my skin, than pretend to be my friend."

"Look how many years it was before a Black man moved into your neighborhood. They had laws against it. Put all us colored folk on the other side of town where there ain't no sidewalks. Up north folks be liberal," he said slipping into street slang that he never used. "I still see that drinking fountain in Alabama. I was so thirsty after driving all day to see family in Huntsville. At a gas station, I went to get a drink of water, the attendant cuffed me and said, 'Boy, don't you read no English? That sign say: "White only." We don't want no nigger germs.'"

Phil continued talking about this deep inexpressible heartache that left him hardened. I could sense his desperation.

Then we fell into a deep silence. We sat at the kitchen table and graded papers together. "Isn't this fun," he said sarcastically. And I thought, "Oh, wouldn't it be, if a white Barbie and Black Ken could sit at the same table and do simple everyday things couples do like grade papers, wash dishes, ride a tandem, dine with neighbors and raise kids."

At school, I divided my class into groups and yelled at the

kids in the blue-eyed group, trying to simulate discrimination. They learned from the experience, but not enough to care about the *others* who lived across the tracks. In the discussion that followed they said things like "'spics are dirty" and "Blacks are lazy and can't be trusted" — all the stereotypical images that had been transferred from parent to child. But when I asked, "do any of you personally know a Black or Mexican teenager?" no one raised his or her hand.

After school, I tried to get in a pick up game with the male staff, but no one would let me play. They would allow a grade school boy to play before they'd let me in the game. When one guy sprained his ankle, I got into the game, but as soon as I stole the ball and scored, they called a water break. When the game started again, they made sure I was on the sideline. I shot baskets alone. I did not know what it felt like to be Black or brown, but, as a woman, I knew the pain and frustration of not being treated as an equal. In the staff room the next day, I signed up to play in the annual student-teacher game.

"You can't play," a teacher insisted. "You're not faculty."

"You mean I'm not male faculty," I retorted, flinging my tennis shoes over my shoulder and striding out of the room, a knife in my gut, my head held high.

When I finished student-teaching, my college coach, Jill Hutchison, offered me a job as third team coach and graduate assistant. But I confessed that I wanted to play in Europe first.

At home in Sterling, I sat in the den, strumming my guitar and contemplating my life. Dad plopped down beside me and drilled me with questions about what was I going to do with my life and I told him that I wanted to go to France."

"It's your life, but you have to consider financial security and your health problems. They don't have chiropractors you can call for a quick fix. Get your foot in the door with a coaching or teaching job."

"I don't want to coach, I want to play," I said sensing my biggest fan withdrawing support for a dream that the rest of the world considered irrational.

The summer after my pro ball gig collapsed, I contemplated pursuing a real career, but the only teaching offer that I had fallen through. So when, as promised, the French coach had called a year later to see if I wanted to play for his team in Paris, I was tempted. I took my frustrations out on the court, but felt like a foreigner inside what had been my home, the gym. I traveled, forced shots, fouled and froze up with fear of failure. What if I wasn't good enough to play in France?

Phil and I ran our usual basketball camps, and when I wasn't at the pool working, I was in the gym. I finished the week by speaking at Illinois State and also at the Eureka College basketball camp in front of a hundred kids. When I recounted my career, I felt like I was reciting pages out of someone else's past. When campers gave me a standing ovation, I blushed. I still thought of myself as being at the bottom of the top, still not good enough. I felt pressure to prove myself—not to Phil, or Dad or Grandpa or my college or community, but to myself. That darn self-pride.

The French coach called and said I would fly over at the end of August. I couldn't even understand the telephone conversation. How would I communicate over there?

I biked 10 miles a day with Phil. I practiced Tae Kwon Do and tried to incorporate that inner calm and the total control of martial arts into my lifestyle. I worked out for hours in the gym and on the track, ignoring the pain in my lower back and the ache in my knees.

"You sure you really want to go to France?" Phil asked.

"I don't know. It may be my last chance."

"If it's a once-in-a-lifetime shot, put something into it. How are you going to get in shape if you're at the lake all summer?"

"I put everything into basketball. For what?"

"You lived and died basketball. Now you're doing nothing. You pretend it doesn't matter, but it's eating away at you."

"I've lost heart. I'll never get in shape."

"You sure it's just not hidden beneath disappointments? Can you accept being at the bottom of the top and work to maintain that position? Even if you don't score, you can make a difference in winning or losing. To go unprepared would make you feel worse than not going at all."

I knew he was right, but a part of me remained so tied to home. "Don't you want me to stay around?"

"Hell no! You belong to the world, not me."

Later, I sat under the oak tree in our front yard and shared my fears with my logical, big brother. "You need to set a goal," Doug said. "If your goal is to go to France, the motivation will return, because the goal is real. If your goal is more to see Europe than to play, then even if things don't work out you will have attained your goal. You can always come home."

"Why couldn't I see that," I said. "Let's go running."

In my heart, I knew all along I would arrive at that decision to go, but I hoped for an out because a part of me was terrified of living abroad. I prayed I'd get a teaching job, but never looked very hard, because I wasn't ready to teach.

I went to Wisconsin, but only for a long weekend—just enough to restore my spirits in the woods where our cabin peeked out from behind evergreens on a lake of glass, that reflected the secrets hidden in my soul.

When I came back from the lake, my goal redefined, I played with greater intensity and I felt an overall sense of well-being that comes from exhaustion. Phil called and asked what I was doing home. I told him that what he had said made sense. I needed to stay in town to train. Every morning, Phil worked out with me in the gym. Ironically, though the school district never offered him the boys' coaching job, they thought he would be just right for coaching the girls' team. I encouraged him to take the offer, though he was skeptical. He wondered why if he wasn't qualified enough to be head coach for the boys' program then how come he was good enough for the girls' team? Same old, same old.

In the afternoon, I biked or swam laps, then returned to the gym for pick up games at night. In the evening I sat on the front porch and strummed my guitar, alone. I wished I could have been happy wearing dresses in 7th grade, make up in 8th, class rings in 9th, that I could have been satisfied having a boyfriend who was All-American instead of having to be the All-American, that I could feel fulfilled by being married, making babies, joining a bridge club. But I had to be different: wear pants to church, laugh when my sweetheart offered his class ring, and play out my dreams on a basketball court long after my classmates started playing house.

I had to go to France and play even if I failed. Most people dream inside so no one can see. I tried my dreams on for size. Like putting my jacket on by myself as a two-year-old, wearing the hood over my tail, as I toddled around the neighborhood. But when the time came to leave my homeland, would I really have the courage to board the plane?

SHS team 1977

Pat SHS 1975

Phil Smith & Pat 1979

pictures from private collection

Asnières team 1980

Marburg 1981 - 1982

pictures from private collection

Games at Illinois State 1976 -1978

photos Courtesy of Dr. JoAnn Rayfield Archives at Illinois State University

Team ISU 1977

photos Courtesy of Dr. JoAnn Rayfield Archives at Illinois State University

Hollywood 1947 Mac & Betty with Jim & Reagan with brother

Mac's testimony dinner NIU 1963

pictures from private collection
courtesy of the Reagan family

Washington DC Touchdwown Club Timmie Award 1982

Coach Mac, Jim & Lenore McKinzie in the Rose Garden
with President Reagan

*pictures from private collection
courtesy of the White House*

Coach Mac
Eureka College 1985

Henry Fields
France 1960s

Paris 1985
Pat, Gérald & baby Nathalie

pictures from private collection

Lechault family, Wisconsin, summer 2012

Ecolint Genève 2001, A Dream Team

Chapter 9: Shooting Hoops in the City of Lights

Paris France 1980-81

*In 1958 FIBA introduces the European Cup
of Women's Championship Clubs, dominated
by the Soviet's legendary 7-foot Uljana
Semjonova, the talisman of Daugawa Riga,
who reigned in the 21-year dynasty of
Russian supremacy in international
basketball.*

FIBA website

"Go on," I said as I hugged my family good-bye at the O'Hare airport, "You can beat the traffic out of here."

"Sure?" dad asked. "We can wait for your boarding call."

"No, I'm fine," I said wiping my eyes with the back of my hand. If they stayed another minute, I would no longer have the courage to leave them.

After losing my contact lens somewhere over the Atlantic, my nerves were frazzled long before we landed in Brussels. I dragged my bags through customs, my heart racing with panic, as I scanned the horde trying to recognize a face I'd never seen before. Just before the terror liquidized into tears, a man, towering above his compatriots, held a sign over his head printed, ASNIÉRES, and yelled, "Potreesha Potreesha-"

Then my new coach, Francis Flamme, whisked me into a BMW and we rolled across the Belgian countryside toward France. I thought my dream to play basketball abroad had come true when my plane touched down in Europe. However, when I saw little people pecking cheeks and scurrying down streets with baseball bats *(baguettes)* slung over their shoulders, it hit me, "Oh my God, I've landed on another planet."

The villages looked like scenes from the pages of picture books. Narrow houses lined winding cobblestone streets where women in wide skirts carried wicker baskets of fruit in one hand and tugged knicker-clad little boys with the other. The hilly, wooded, emerald countryside dotted with stone fences and sheep farms reminded me of Wisconsin. After four hours, we rolled to a stop in front of a miniature duplex that looked like a dollhouse. I feared if I breathed too hard, I'd break the elegant décor. After a meal of sausages and bread, Francis explained in broken English that soon we'd be having dinner.

"Dinner? I thought that was dinner."

"No, just an entrée."

"But I'm not hungry. I just want to sleep."

"No *problème*," Francis said.

My hostess, the club secretary and former player, led me up a spiral staircase and showed me to a room the size of a walk-in closet. She set a towel and a dish of fruit by the bed and whispered, "*Bonne nuit.*" I slept for the next twenty hours.

During breakfast, I sat on the patio, admiring the scenery, sipping tea in a china cup and feeling like a foreign ambassador. We went shopping in L'Isle Adam, a northern suburb of Paris. We bought a roast at the butcher's, pastry at the bakery, peaches at the fruit stand, and sole at the fish market. I pointed and giggled as my hostess and I looked up words in a pocket dictionary.

That evening, I woke up at midnight unable to sleep, haunted by the pictures of the giant women Francis had shown me in basketball books. I thought the French were petite. I feared that if I didn't measure up, they'd send me back home.

On Sunday, the basketball club president came to dinner. For six hours, I smiled and nodded and tried to understand the conversation during the endless meal. First we drank the apéritif, a licorice flavored Pastis. Then wine and fish. Wine and meat. Wine and cheese. Wine and fruit. Then dessert and champagne. I stared at my glass and debated what to do with the scarlet liquid. I grew up in a coach's family, where drinking was taboo. How could I imbibe alcohol in front of my coach? Nonetheless to avoid offending the hostess I tipped the wine to my lips at regular intervals. Much to my alarm, when my glass was half empty, Francis filled it again.

After the dinner, they showed me Paris by night. I stared out the window wide-eyed at the world-famous Eiffel Tower, Arch of Triumph, Notre Dame church. Paris aglow by night made Washington D.C. look like a wide spot in the road.

On Monday morning, Francis drove me to my studio, across from a factory on a side street in Courbevoie, a northwestern suburb, just four metro stops or a five-minute train ride from the Saint-Lazare station in Paris. Francis stocked my cupboards with the American staples of bread, jelly, juice, milk and Coca-Cola® in the original, six-ounce bottles.

My first few days were a whirlwind of long, four-hour dinners with players and people associated with the team. At the end of every meal my stomach ached from the new foods; my head pounded from the new words. Out of shape from so much eating, I decided to run one morning. I jogged down the cobblestone street inhaling the aroma of citrus fruits and fresh croissants, past the green grocers, bakery, and baby boutique, toward the park. I ran laps around the fountains and up and down the stairs between the gardens of magenta and gold. When I returned to my apartment, I shook the key, rattled the handle, kicked the door, and then ran back into the street waving my arms like a lunatic. A man stopped.

"*Je ne parle pas Français*," I said. "Locked out!" I pointed to my key.

"*Je ne comprend pas*," he said.

I motioned for him to follow me. He chuckled as he unlocked the door with a twist of his wrist. Once inside, I slumped to the floor shaking.

Every day I ran, showered, then returned to the park to people watch. Old men in suit jackets and berets played the national pastime, *boules*, tossing large metal balls at a smaller one in a game like marbles for adults. Toddlers, in starched clothes played on the slides while mothers sat on park benches, their tongues clicking as fast as their knitting needles. Old ladies fed the pigeons and gossiped. I envied their ability to engage in small talk.

Each day was a test of endurance. No one spoke English. What was language without meaning; what was humanness without language? My hand trembled as I unlocked my mailbox every morning, hoping there would be a letter from home, a reminder that I existed, that I hadn't dropped off the planet.

Christine Wachowiak, the first teammate I met, was an 18-year-old Junior national team guard from a village near Metz. Over dinner at a pizza place, I smiled at the pretty, blonde girl. I couldn't understand the conversation, but I saw Christine's mom put her arm around her, her dad pat her knee, and her brother wink. I understood the unspoken love and pain in saying farewell.

Our first practice almost never started. All twelve players greeted one another by kissing each other on the cheeks four times. My hands shook when I saw the imposing stature of our two centers. During the workout, our two French superstars kept sitting down. Christine, nicknamed Kiki, seeing the shock in my eyes, whispered, "They old. Have babies."

Asnières Sport had the league's two best "*pivots*" (French term for centers). Françoise Quiblier, 27 years old, played in 182 international selection games. Elisabeth Riffiold, age 33, with 247 international selections, earned seven French titles during her career. The former was a dark-haired, prima donna; the latter, a selfless team player. One friend, one foe. Both had children, which astounded me. In the States, women's professional sports and motherhood seemed incompatible.

Perhaps due to personality or proximity in living arrangements, I became closer to Elisabeth. At the French National Institute for Sports and Physical Education (INSEP) Sport University, Elisabeth met Issa Diaw, the men's Senegalese high jump champion. They lived in the apartment building next to me and always welcomed me in their home.

The couple made a striking contrast, a 6'3" blonde French woman and the handsome, coal Black African. In the States interracial relationships were taboo; I was surprised at how easily they were accepted in French society. Elisabeth said she never experienced bigotry because of her mixed-race relationship. "As athletes, we were given a free pass," she said. "Playing basketball was my full-time job and I was paid by France to train and compete."

Elisabeth invited me over for couscous and other African specialties, so I was only too happy to babysit their hyperactive 2-year-old son, Martin. After spending a few hours chasing Martin, I understood why the moms on the team needed to sit down during practice. Elisabeth, a versatile center with a sweet shot, gained recognition for being the first French woman to shoot the jumper, a skill she said that she learned at age 20 from watching tapes of the Boston Celtic's Bill Russell.

Later Elisabeth would pass on that gift to her sons, the younger one, Boris Diaw, close friend of Tony Parker, would go on to star in the NBA. Neither son loved basketball until the 1992 Barcelona Olympics, when the United States Dream Team sparked international interest.

Martin's enthusiasm rubbed off on his younger brother. "I think he identified with Black American players much more than with a blonde French mother," Elisabeth said of Martin, who played professionally in France's second division. Boris, formed in the European club system like his mom, went on to become one of the premier French players in the NBA.

In France, only club, not school teams, existed. Players on our first division team ranged in age from 16 to 33.

After practice Francis asked if I would rather live with Kiki, than alone. I welcomed the companionship and moved into Kiki's flat in a low-rent, 12-story high rise in the industrial suburb, Argenteuil, farther north of Paris. After World War II, France was hit with housing shortages, so architects designed concrete housing projects for workers. In the 1960s, the government welcomed immigrants to fill manpower shortages in the rapidly expanding economy. Argenteuil, part of the new *banlieue*, French equivalent of ghetto, was still safe in the early 1980s. The gaudy orange walls were an inexpensive attempt to illuminate the dreary apartment, which consisted of the bare essentials of a kitchen, living room, and two bedrooms. After I arranged clothes in a cupboard, I collapsed on my single bed.

We woke up to a bell ringing. Elisabeth was at the door yelling, "Hurry up!" We had overslept for our first road trip. When we met the caravan of cars driving us to Belgium, we repeated the greeting ritual. Etiquette at 6:30 a.m. I grumbled as we kissed cheeks under a street lamp. Then I hopped in Francis's car and we drove through Paris, as the early morning mist rose from the Arch of Triumph and the deserted Champs Elysees looked surreal as in a dream.

Near the border, Francis asked, "You have your passport?"

"Passport? No, what do I need my passport for?"

"*La douane*! Customs!" he said, then swore and pulled the car off the side of the road. "*Dehors*! Out."

Francis's face turned crimson; I feared he would abandon me on the roadside. Instead, he opened the trunk and pointed at it, and insisted, "You! In!" I crawled in and folded my long limbs into a ball. I could imagine the morning news headlines, "American superstar asphyxiated when smuggled across the border in the boot of a car."

We arrived at the game an hour late and when I entered the game, I was still so rattled from the ride in the trunk that my hands shook. I felt like a freshman again. Kiki came in off the bench and whispered, "No pass. Shoot."

I swished the next ten shots. As soon as I cut our opponents' lead, I fed our big girls in the post to avoid the wrath. At Francis's pre-game talk before our second match, I nodded even though I never understood a word he said. I wanted to play well to show my appreciation for being allowed out of the trunk. We beat the team from Holland in the final. The statistician rushed over to me with his book of stats and pointed to the numbers, 28 points, 18 rebounds, 10 assists. The teams stood together for the awards ceremony. When Françoise walked forward to get our team trophy, I wanted to cheer and hug everyone like I used to do in the States, but no one else appeared happy. When they announced, *"Numéro dix, Patreesha Mackencee, meilleure joueuse du tournoi,"* I had no idea what they were talking about. A pair of hands pushed me forward to accept the most valuable player trophy. I smiled as I shook hands with the announcer, then turned to face my teammates' cold stares. I looked down longing to crawl under the floorboards and shoved the trophy in the bottom of my sport bag. When the team went out to celebrate, I lingered in the team bunkroom, choking back tears.

Later, I forced myself to join the others in the bar, a standard fixture in European gyms where sports were as social as they were competitive. The after-game drink was as much a part of the ritual as the post-match shower. In the bar, submerged in a cloud of smoke, my teammates leaned on the table listening to Françoise's story. Just as I sat down, they burst out laughing. Living in a foreign country was like always being the only one who doesn't get the joke.

As though I was going through a second childhood, every experience was new and different. Like words to a baby the language had no meaning. Everything I saw I asked, *"Qu'est ce que c'est ?"* (what is it?) I spoke in simple words and broken phrases with the vocabulary of a 2-year-old.

There was so much I couldn't understand, like a general strike, the Frenchman's birthright. I waited an hour for the metro before I figured out it wasn't working, then took another line and got lost. I wandered the streets of Paris crying invisible tears, scanning throngs for a familiar face.

I dragged myself to practice, but when Kiki ran up to kiss me, I managed to grin. The younger players were happy to see me and enthusiastic in practice; however, my older teammates remained distant. In the middle of practice, Françoise stopped the play to yell at me. I was astounded. Never before had a teammate spoken to me in that way. Only the coach yelled in an American practice. I looked over at Francis; he looked away as if she scared him, too. Françoise with her thick-muscled, solid stature and dark mane would be running the team. As her incessant criticism continued, my play lapsed from mediocre to poor until finally Francis excused me to the showers. I stood under the hot mist and cried.

After practice, teammates shocked me by drinking champagne to celebrate the season's debut with a group of fans. By the time we got back to my apartment, my throat ached. Kiki clucked her tongue and said, "Wear a scarf when it's drafty like I told you, then you won't get sick."

"Drink this," she said, handing me a glass of hot orange juice and a plate of yogurt and mashed bananas. Her old-fashioned remedies couldn't heal, but like a grandma's outdated cures, they brought comfort.

When I woke up the next morning, I felt like I'd swallowed a baseball. I dozed off through the day. I received letters from friends saying how much they envied me experiencing things most people only dream of, but I longed for home. People saw me from afar, admiring my grace as I floated across the sky, but would they still be so envious if they knew that all that kept me afloat was hot air?

Empty days stretched before me like a desert. I woke up, ate breakfast, washed dishes, cleaned, wrote in my journal, jogged, and played guitar. I interacted with no one until the 5:00 p.m. practice where I was reprimanded by the coach and scolded by teammates. I felt so unwelcome in France. No one could understand why the American, raised with a basketball in her arms, dribbled off her toe, missed the rim, threw the ball away, and could no longer play the game she was born to play.

One of the hardest parts about playing ball in a foreign land was never knowing what was going on. Without the language skill, I went into every game clueless about the opponent. Though I suspect the coaches had little experience formulating scouting reports, seasoned players knew how to defend opponents. Elisabeth and Françoise had played in the Olympics and for countless other national select teams and understood their rivals' moves and style of play.

Our first official season game was in Japy, the oldest gym in Paris against Racing, another Division I team. The ball wouldn't bounce back up when you dribbled off the floorboards that were warped and blackened from a century of dirt. Before the game, I felt flat. How could I get psyched about playing in an antique gym, in front of strangers, with teammates that wouldn't quit yelling at me? I pretended my dad and grandpa were in the stands, inspiring my play. Just before tip-off, I followed my usual ritual and jogged off the court to find what Europeans call the WC (water closet). I entered the door at one end of the gym marked *toilettes*, but when I opened the stall door I saw two blocks of cement over a small a hole filled with running water. Red-faced, I laughed thinking I had walked into the men's room. Then I entered the door labeled toilettes at the other end of the gym, where I bumped into a man standing at the urinal. Alas, women too, were obliged to squat over an ice fishing hole, known in France as a Turkish toilet.

At tip off, as I shook hands with our opponents, I felt nervous excitement. The game had barely begun when Françoise yelled, "*Pas si vite* (not so fast)."

"Slow down," I thought, "on a fast break!" I continued playing at my American speed, and she yelled, "*Temps mort.*"

Francis called a time-out and repeated, "Slow down."

But when the point guard came down on the fast break and hit me off on the left wing, I took my shot.

"*Passes le ballon*," Françoise screamed after I hit three straight jump shots.

"I'll pass *le ballon* (the ball) when you get your lazy ass down court," I thought. Our center loafed, but wanted the play to begin only after she was set up in shooting position. Later, Françoise yelled at me for missing her on a pass and stood by the bench pouting until Francis replaced her. Even if she was a superstar of France, no player in America would get away with the stuff she pulled. In the second half, to appease our spoiled *enfant*, Francis moved me to center, so that Françoise could play wing like she wanted.

"But I don't play center," I said.

"*Oui pivot*," he yelled. "*Les Americaines* play anywhere."

So I cut across the lane, crashed the boards and took a beating. After the game, my new white uniform looked gray from hitting the dirt, flattened by the physical French players. When officials never called even the most flagrant fouls, I realized what Francis was talking about when he said they had the home court advantage. When the final buzzer rang, my lower back throbbed. Why was I playing in a street ball league with a condition that could impair me for the rest of my life?

Francis was such a nice guy that I wondered if he was too nice to be a coach, but his love of basketball was parallel to none. Later he became the successful President of Paris-Levallois men's basketball club, as well as serve as the Director General of the *Fédération Française de Basket-ball* from 1983-2007. He remains on the committee today.

One of the biggest differences between basketball in the States and that overseas was officiating—or lack thereof. In France, games felt like semi-organized brawls and players were allowed much more physical contact under the boards and in the frontcourt. I often wondered why the local girls played. They worked until 6:00 p.m. at day jobs, and then trained at night. The solvent club sponsors, like Asnières, funded by a company that made street cleaning equipment, provided employment for players within the company. Several of my teammates like Kiki worked as secretaries in the company. Our coach also worked for them in the front office. The top French Division I clubs like Stade Français or Clermont-Ferrand could recruit the best national players by offering small salaries or stipends or perks like apartments.

The easy practices made me more restless. One day a week, we endured shooting practice, launching 100 shots over an upright bench. Every morning, I bent over our bathtub washing our workout clothes, yet felt guilty that I didn't have to work like the rest of my teammates. I was the human machine replacing conveniences lacking in a French household *sans* garbage disposal, dishwasher, and microwave. Our refrigerator, the size of a portable TV, was so tiny, daily shopping was required. Every night Kiki came home and scolded if I forgot to buy bread or milk. I wanted to work for a living and go to bed at night feeling I'd accomplished something.

As if playing charades, I acted out others' lives searching for a suitable role. Like a chameleon, I adapted to the situation. Most weekends Kiki's family visited. My heart ached as I watched Kiki and her beau cuddling on the couch or hugging over the morning coffee. Even in my apartment, I felt like an intruder. Living in a foreign country was like being a guest in someone else's home.

I had always turned to my family for emotional support. I longed just to hear their voices; however, without a phone, the only time I could speak to my parents was during a monthly phone call from our sponsor's office. Therefore, I depended on snail mail. When I felt like I couldn't go on, I would receive a thin blue airmail envelope full of encouragement from home.

I hated being dependent on my teammates for interpreting and transportation. On the weekend, I insisted Kiki teach me to drive our 1959 pumpkin orange, two door Citroën, a cardboard box on wheels. It looked like I could fold up the French *deux chevaux* (2 horses) and park it in my pocket. Kiki screamed as I weaved across the country roads struggling to get my foot off the clutch and onto the gas before the car stalled. I had never driven a 4-speed before and couldn't understand her instructions in French. Paris was no place to learn how to maneuver a stick shift, especially a manual one stuck in the dashboard.

I shifted gears, the car coughed, sputtered, stalled. "Oops, peel your face off the windshield, Kiki."

"*Arrête! Le feu est rouge!*" (Stop! The light is red.)

"What red light?"

"Oh, no, Potreesha, I take you where you *désires!*"

I must learn, I insisted while Kiki scolded, wiped the sweat off her brow and swore in the seat next to me. We bumped along, like on Mr. Toad's wild ride, while the rolling hills flew past our window.

After a few weeks of nerve-racking lessons, Kiki let me drive the car alone. I would have arrived at my destination faster on foot, because whenever I came into a roundabout where a half a dozen roads merged like the spokes of a wheel, I froze. The car approaching from the right has the right of away, but I was afraid to enter the circle. I waited for all the cars to pass while a line of irate drivers piled up behind me.

Everything about living in a foreign country became stressful, even simple tasks like driving, grocery shopping, and mailing letters. I wasn't surprised the next morning when I awoke with my fourth sore throat. My throat felt raw for a few days, then the pain subsided but my glands stayed swollen and I remained exhausted. The doctor thought I had mononucleosis because my spleen and glands were enlarged, but the blood tests were inconclusive. I assumed my imagined illness, my depression, and my chronic fatigue were a self-imposed phenomenon that came from feeling useless. The doctor prescribed white pills that he called vitamins, but vitamins don't contain caffeine. My life was in a bottle and my days were being dispensed at the nearest pharmacy.

Trips to away games were my only distraction. We flew to Marseilles and took a bus to Toulon for our game the next night. We arrived late, but the team insisted on eating their regular five-course pre-game meal. As they devoured the steak and potatoes forty-five minutes before the game, I picked at my food, trying to explain that we never eat less than four hours before a game. For my teammates, a perk of playing club ball was the multi-course, pre-game meal on road trips.

Francis told me not to warm up because he wouldn't play me unless he had to. By half we were down by ten points, so I popped a pill the doctor prescribed for energy. My legs, like lead weights, forced me to slow down on my shot, so instead of shoving the ball, I released it with a nice soft touch. I helped cut the lead and in the last 20 seconds we were ahead by three. Then a teammate committed a stupid foul. They scored a free throw, stole the ball from our guard, and the game ended in a tie. I walked back toward our bench thinking it would be overtime, but the team headed for the locker room.

"Aren't we going to finish the game?" I asked Francis.

"It's over."

"But the score!" I said pointing to the board, 76-76.

"We should have won," Francis lamented. I kicked the bench in fury. Only in France could they end a game in a tie. On the way home, my teammates were sure I'd recovered from my illness because I scored so many points. I could never begin to explain the American competitive mentality. I had played with a broken finger, twisted back, inflamed knee; I would never let a sore throat keep me off the court. Yes, I did still feel sick. In fact, I felt sicker. Part of my chronic fatigue came from the misunderstandings that arose.

As part of the European Cup, we played our first game against Vigo, Spain, in front of our home crowd. In the warm-up, I was pumped, but after I missed my first two shots, Françoise started to yell at me, then at Francis. Sure enough, Francis repeated her orders to me, too. Too late. I'd already hit three in a row. I ignored criticism and played my style. Soon my high fives were contagious and in the second half the whole bench was cheering. Every game we had four or five players in double figures and I began to think maybe this was finally my dream to be on a balanced team like my sister Karen's state championship high school squad. We were excited after we won as we were assured of seeing at least three other countries.

A week later, we flew to Madrid, and then boarded a bus to Vigo for the return match. In the countryside, men pulled tractors by hand through the fields, and the women washed clothes in the creek; whereas in the city, the poverty was hidden. The gym with a linoleum floor was comparable to French gyms. The score of the game seesawed back and forth and in the end we lost by a point. I collapsed on the floor, devastated, while my teammates jumped and shouted jubilantly.

"Patreezia," Francis screamed pulling me off the floor. "We win! We played Vigo home, win two points. Play away, lose one point. We win! One point ahead."

I looked at him dumbfounded. To determine who advances to the next round of the European Cup, they calculated the point differential. After the game, we had dinner with the Spaniards. Both teams danced together like one big family and my heart ached with a longing for my own people, my own land, and my own identity. They wanted me to sing an American song, so together we shouted Old MacDonald and swayed arm and arm. The little, dark-skinned, dark-eyed Spanish coach and I communicated with the sparkle in our eyes. We tried to express our mutual attraction for one another's manner, customs, and spirit. He handed me a piece of paper with a drawing of a heart that said, our heart *"parler"* the same language. For once, I felt connected to the entire human race.

Back on the court, I felt lost. The game, which I once played as naturally as I breathed, became foreign. The first half I dragged up and down the court, flat as an open Pepsi left in the refrigerator for a week. At half time I popped energy pills, and the second half I raced down the court, out of control like a maniac. We won and were in first place in France.

Between games, the City of Lights offered an unlimited diversion. But basketball tormented me, especially when, without any explanation, the coach decided not to play me in the next game. In a rage that night at the team dinner, I ordered wine for the first time. While everyone looked on disapprovingly, I mellowed out. The double standard. The French drank wine with their meals and partied, but American professionals had to live by the rules that everyone else ignored.

To pick up my failing spirits, I invited the team for Thanksgiving dinner. For three days, I trampled a well-worn path between my apartment and the supermarket. I went to the butcher's and asked for a turkey. He gave me a slice of meat.

"*No, je veux tout l'oiseau*" I said. "Give me the whole bird," and I flapped my arms like wings. He shook his head in amazement and said he'd order one for me. I spent hours in the kitchen pouring over recipe books; I didn't know how to broil a steak, let alone a whole turkey dinner. I realized too late that my teammates mistook, *Fête américaine*, to mean dance party, not full course dinner. When my teammates arrived, their eyes popped out at the sight of a Tom turkey sitting at the head of the table. They wanted to eat the dishes of corn, potatoes, salads, in courses; I tried to explain they must pile their plates full with everything at once — the American way.

Francis brought champagne and I toasted them, "When I arrived in France, I was like a pilgrim, you all shared what you had with me. Now it was my turn to thank you."

Then everyone engaged in their rapid-fire French conversations and I felt exasperated because I couldn't understand them. How was I to go about celebrating a special national American holiday in a foreign country when my family was a continent away?

After dinner, my best friends remained. We plugged in the radio and danced. Then they asked me to play the guitar and we sang and laughed. As they kissed me goodnight twice on each cheek, I glowed. Maybe they got my message after all.

Still, I wondered if I really existed? I floated through the cloudy, wet winter days in a stupor, drifting in and out of illusions, living in dreams of home. How sensitive one becomes when one sees the world through tears. I was torn between two worlds, here and now in France, and the before and after in the U.S.A. If I had never known another world, perhaps I could adjust, but I had another life. I felt like I had died and nobody came to the funeral. Worse yet, no one knew I was gone. I woke up in the morning filled with the dread of facing another day. Everyone needs a purpose.

What was I doing here? Surely, it was not just to play basketball. Paris lost its novelty. When I saw pictures of the Eiffel Tower, I couldn't believe I was living there. I reread the part of my hospital journal where a man called from France offering me a job, the day after my doctors' whispered surgery. Did I forget there was a day I couldn't walk? In the hospital I realized how much I needed my health, now I realized how much I needed my family. They wrote that my courage kept them going; I drew strength from their letters. I was the gutless wanderer, the adventuresome homebody.

No one said, "Pat don't be a fool and go to France where you might starve, might get injured, might be miserable." Everyone said, "Go for it." Here I was again chasing another rainbow, and just when I thought I'd reached the pot of gold at the end, I found it was all an illusion.

"I hope you aren't changing too fast for the rest of us," Sue wrote. But I was just catching up. Would I always feel so driven? Mom, please tell me is this a stage that I will outgrow? In childhood, she kissed my skinned knees, patched up my favorite blue jeans, and sent me back outside. In adulthood, Mom honored my uniqueness and urged me to follow my own star.

"Maybe you overlooked your real purpose," my mom wrote. "We are all learning so much about France from you."

As my game improved, I felt for fleeting moments like I belonged. But most of the time I felt restless and useless. At those times, I would eat, finding some superficial solace in a stuffed stomach. On sleepless nights, I sought consolation in a cookie. Then, as if obsessed by my figure, which I had learned to take pride in, I worried about gaining weight. A finger down my throat terminated my anxiety-induced eating binges. As I hung over a toilet bowl behind a closed door, I wondered if others saw through my charade and knew I was not nearly as together as I pretended.

The weekly game helped me retain some semblance of sanity, but drove me crazy at times. But at least it gave me a social life. After the game, players came over for crêpes. Unlike many American men, French guys from the men's team, comfortable in the kitchen, flipped crêpes and filled them with meat, cheese, or marmalade. After dinner, I played the guitar. Everyone sang or screamed in English until the flesh on my fingers turned raw, and then we turned on the radio and danced. We topped off the night with coffee. Partying here was real. Nobody got drunk, nobody rushed to the bedroom to cop a feel, and nobody went home feeling they'd missed the fun.

"Hey, can you believe we're here?" I said slapping Kiki the high five as we boarded the tour bus in Prague.

"What a miserable life," she said scrunching up her nose.

"They're so poor."

"No one smiles in the shops. Maybe it's because of the dreary weather." But it wasn't only the clouds. Hunger and despair flickered in the people's dark eyes. We felt guilty buying the bargain-priced leather and jewelry when the locals couldn't afford to purchase meat. The aisles of the grocery were bare and the shops somber. Beautiful buildings lined Prague's boulevards, but I would remember scowling faces under black garments, people trudging through snow with their heads down.

That night we lost the game and I was so disappointed. If we had beaten Prague, we'd have gone to Russia. One point away from Moscow and my dream to play against the legendary 7-foot Semjonova. Since its inception in 1950, the Soviet Union won every final of the biannual Euro Basket Championship except the first year and in 1958 when they were upset by Bulgaria. (The Soviet Union claimed 21 titles, 17 consecutive until 1991, a year during which both the Soviet Union and Yugoslavia collapsed.)

After our loss in Prague, I wanted to be left alone. Instead, we had to eat dinner with our opponents, a drab affair held in our hotel. Afterwards I wandered to a meeting room where men at a business convention argued and knocked back shots of vodka. They offered me a drink, so I sat down. We communicated in broken French and English, with the men who were more versed in other languages interpreting Czech. When they found out I was American, they wanted to know what I thought of communism. I was surprised that instead of abhorring their imposing government, they were as proud of their country as we were of ours.

In April, the pressure mounted in the French Cup play-off games at the end of the season. In our next home game, I tossed a desperate last second shot. The ball swirled around the rim, then fell in the net, swishing at the beep of the buzzer.

"The basket? Ref. Count it."

The ref waved his hands, signaling no basket.

"Francis, protest the call! I released the shot before the buzzer!"

Francis shrugged, like there was no hope, like he wanted

the season to be over. I couldn't believe officials were screwing us on our own home court, not in France. While opponents celebrated, I stared at the final score in disbelief, Asnières 88, Clermont 89. I gazed straight ahead, stupefied, my eyes fixed in place, completely stoic. I shook my opponents' hands and walked toward the locker room. We had gotten knocked out of the French national championship final and my teammates were talking about what they were going to eat for dinner.

When Françoise started to tell me why I got that traveling call in the first half, I glared back at her. When I stepped out of the locker room, Francis said, "Good game."

But I walked out of the gym, dejected. Even my finest performance, was never enough. I was convinced my purpose here was to help my team win the championship in France, but this country wasn't weaned on competitiveness like mine. Win, lose or draw, in France it's all the same. Just a game. But I was raised in a different country, culture, and clan; I was conditioned to be a winner. It didn't merely sting to lose; it crucified a dream.

I walked into the parking lot in a stupor. A horn honked and a car swerved to miss hitting me. A teammate rolled down the window and yelled, "Look out," she shouted, "I want you to meet André and Gérald."

I started to say hello. When I looked in the back seat, a handsome, dark-haired guy grinned. I did a double-take and smiled back thinking I knew him, then blushed realizing we'd never met before. After that game, I was sure no one could make me smile; yet suddenly I glowed.

A few weeks later, when that same teammate invited me to dinner with friends, I secretly hoped Gérald would be one of those friends. When we knocked at the apartment door, he answered. I felt the same breathlessness I used to feel in high school when my secret crush said hello in the hall. I wanted to talk to him, but a half a dozen people separated us. Instead we spoke with our eyes. As the evening wore on, the wine wore off the resistance. In broken French/English we exchanged those trivial details that everyone shares on their first encounter. After dinner we drove to St. Germain and strolled down the Parisian streets. He slipped his arm around me as though it belonged there. On the street corner as we waited for the changing lights, he leaned over and kissed me. I stiffened like a schoolgirl on her first date.

When the night drew to a close, he whispered, *"Viens chez moi, ce soir."*

"Non, pas ce soir," I fought off the most natural human response and refused on the American principle, never go home with a man on the first date. I didn't want love to unravel my neatly packaged life again. He gave me his number and told me to call. I thought I'd throw the note away; instead I dialed his number from a phone booth on the corner, the next day.

"Allo," I stammered and before I said a word, he'd recognized my voice and demanded, "When can I see you?"

"This afternoon, I guess," I said.

"And tonight?"

"No, tonight I'm not free," I had a game, then a party, and then a date. My hand shook as I hung up the receiver. I'd been too nervous to explain where I lived. When he rang my doorbell just twenty minutes later, I was astounded.

I bustled about the kitchen baking for Kiki's party. While I watched the cookies brown, he watched me blush. Kiki came home and invited him to the party. I uninvited him. His penetrating brown eyes stared at me as if I should drop everything to make room for him in my life.

"Promise you'll come for lunch tomorrow, then."

"Okay," I said as I spilled coffee on my jeans.

At the door, he kissed me good-bye and our bodies seemed the same height; I had gotten used to being with ultra tall basketball players, Gérald, at 6'1" seemed short. Finally, he left my apartment, but not my mind. The evening party was spoiled by memories of him and I picked a fight with the basketball player I had been dating.

The next day I felt as excited as a child at Christmas as I drove toward Gérald's apartment, only a block from my first apartment. There was a note on his door, "You just reached the jackpot, all you have to do is ring." I rang and so it was.

Instead of the customary greeting, rather than a kiss, handshake, or all American hug, Gérald opened the door and embraced me with his eyes, looking at me as though I were everything in the world. For that moment, I was. Mesmerized by his eyes, I found myself melting around him. Like caramel coating an apple, I turned to taffy in his arms.

The days that followed became a blur of *vin blanc, dîner pour deux,* and *l'amour toute la nuit.* (white wine, dinner for two and love all night.)Whatever emotions couldn't be expressed in his faulty English or my broken French, he compensated with a stare that left me speechless. Though I knew I had to return to my home country, I remained, spellbound. Every day, I'd leave for the States in my mind, but at I night I'd find myself locked in, imprisoned by his eyes. Reality told me I must go home; dreams told me I was home.

I was terrified of my feelings. Gérald was so French. Broad shoulders, firm from life, not weight-lifting, tapered to slender hips, Gérald's fine European build was a reflection of his fine French culture where quality not quantity counts. I knew he loved the sound of rock and roll, the taste of fresh dairy cream, the sensation of soft fingers across his back. In the morning I'd see him leaving for work in a pressed shirt and tie, in the afternoon I'd hear him cajoling with the butcher, in the night, I'd feel him reach for me in his dreams. I knew his body like my own, but his mind, like his eyes, remained a mysterious cavern. I couldn't begin to share his passion for film, politics, and literature. What could we share? The daily weather report, morning coffee, afternoon tea, evening martini. Like a bedtime story, we read silently to ourselves, living each in our own separate worlds, coming together only in gazes.

I felt I had to overcome this infatuation. After being with Gérald for a few days, I would get away from him, trying to distance my feelings. But when we were apart, I found myself craving him. I ate hardboiled eggs at midnight, bread at 1 a.m., and cookies at 2 a.m. One night, I devoured a package of madeleines; hard, dried cakes, then leaned over the toilet bowl heaving. A pair of imaginary eyes stared back at me in laughing mockery, asking why I would make myself vomit. I was lovesick.

While Gérald and his friends discussed world affairs in a Parisian restaurant, I sipped wine and waited for the warm mellowing effect to overcome me.

"*Vous est*" (you is,) I started to say, wanting to enter the conversation with my viewpoint.

"*Vous êtes,*" (you are,) Gérald corrected me and as my face reddened, I realized I had forgotten my point. The heated debate could not wait for a foreigner to grapple with the grammar. A stupid mistake. Even I knew better. I was so busy formulating my theory; I hadn't worked out the correct French pronunciation. While the discussion grew livelier, I sipped wine and remained silent. My language skills never mattered with the ball players since we communicated on a simple level, but with Gérald, an intellectual, I shared his embarrassment at my accent and his exasperation at my limited vocabulary. I drank to escape the moment, a culmination of all moments in France. I didn't at this time, or any other, really fit in.

Basketball didn't help bolster my self-esteem. The French Basketball Federation was banning all foreign non-European female players from the league, so I would have to leave. They wanted to avoid the invasion of Americans like in the men's league where entire starting line ups were composed of my compatriots. I took it as a personal rebuff. Only friendly matches remained, but I could barely drag myself through the games.

I felt ashamed. *Oui, j'aime la vie à Paris, tous les gens sont gentils, tout va bien.* (Yes, I love the life in Paris, it's beautiful, everyone is nice, everything is going well.) I was a farce. All that remained was the pedestal, the statue, the monument, the shrine. I wanted to tell all the boys and girls that a search for the sense of self in a little round ball was impossible. When the final buzzer sounded all that was left was emptiness, even in victory, a perpetual frustration that no matter how well you played, it was never good enough. You try to measure your worth, the intangible soul, against the tangible game. Sport is consistent. Someone wins; someone loses. But the soul, the self is infinite. To let the game reflect the self is a terrible injustice. I knew because for the last six years, I had seen myself only in statistics. The season ended, as all seasons must. I knew I couldn't play forever; I couldn't continue to measure my self-worth by the bounce of a ball.

Self-discipline, an athlete's greatest asset, left me mid-season and all that remained was empty despair. In listless misery, I tried to reawaken my old self. But the relief was only temporary. I wanted the freedom to party like a non-athlete and rejected the double standard. I sought the same liberties as a male, but I discovered real freedom came from choice. I chose a chemical-free life because I wanted to be in control, determined to recover self-discipline by setting a new goal.

Even with Gérald, the only time of day when I was content was the early morning before I was awake, when he pressed his warm body next to mine and we folded together. Then he kissed my cheek and whispered, *"Je t'aime."* I enviously watched him dress for work. I heard the coffee perk, the shower run, the door shut, closing me in dreams of a playroom, double car garage, and a dog in the yard.

But when I was fully awake, my dreams turned to reality. I paced the apartment like a caged animal, the pet wife. Two steps to the john, three to the den, four to the kitchen. I drank coffee by the pot full, swept the floor, washed the dishes, all of which consumed mere minutes of that monster, time. I thought I should call the neighbor and invite her for tea. Then I remembered I had no neighbors that spoke my language. Some mornings Gérald called, some afternoons he came for lunch. I undercooked the rice and overcooked the meat and shared pieces of my fragmented self with a stranger.

I existed in two worlds. Was I becoming two people? I longed to go home, yet wanted to stay. I ran helter-skelter in search of a new dream to fill up my empty void. When my agent called to ask if I was interested in playing in Germany, I thought "Start over again? Are you crazy?" but answered, "yes" and boarded the train.

I slouched in the orange vinyl seat, staring out the window at the green hills, thinking my life, like the train, just kept rolling along. A controller in a green uniform spoke in a harsh guttural voice. I handed him my passport. We crossed the border to Germany as simply as crossing a state line. When the train stopped at Marburg, I got off and looked around the empty station for my agent, a man I never even knew existed until he called offering me a job in Germany.

My heart beat faster and I began to sweat. When I was sure that there was no one to meet me, I sat down on the bench and took out my notebook. To calm my rising fear, I would pretend that this was happening to a character. But, my hand shook so much that my writing was illegible. I went into a gift shop to ask what time it was and the salesgirl answered.

"*Es ist drei Uhr.*" (It is 15:00 p.m.)

"*Je ne comprends pas,*" I said, using French to tell her I didn't understand what she said, and she shrugged. I repeated the same thing in English at the newsstand. Who was the fool who told me all the Germans speak English? Who was the bigger fool that believed him? I picked up the telephone, but the only response I got with my francs was a dull buzz. I had no Deutsch marks and couldn't even say hello in this foreign language. I paced next to the tracks. The train conductor signaled to me. I walked over to talk; when I explained my plight, he just shrugged.

I pointed to the phone and said, "Telephone."

He pointed to the booth and said, "Telephone."

Our conversation developed no farther. I pointed to the station clock, which read military time 15:00. Five o'clock? I told my agent my train arrived at 5 p.m. The stationmaster showed me his wristwatch: the time read 3 p.m. I had confused military time with standard time. When 5 p.m. finally arrived though, I still saw no mystery man. I bent over to tie my shoe. When I looked up, a beer-bellied man in a polo shirt, shorts, and sandals extended a sweaty palm and said, "Patreezia."

With a cigar in one hand and an ice cream cone in the other, he talked too fast. Fast talkers were like contracts in small print. I disliked this guy from the moment he opened his mouth and wondered how he could OWN me when I didn't even know he existed. After college, I had filled out a form requesting my statistics and inquiring if I was interested in playing in Europe. The word agent was never mentioned. Now this crook made money off my back. He drove me to dinner in his cheap imitation sports car where we met the gaunt-faced team manager, Peter. I devoured a fat sausage, sipped warm beer and ignored my "agent" who was selling my body.

Peter took me to the tennis club to meet other people associated with the team. When my agent wasn't around, I smiled. I could do my own selling. They took me to a gym with a tile floor. I raced down the court with new players: Anja, Helga, Babetta all of whose names sounded as foreign as their language. After five minutes, I was bored. I encouraged the others and passed the ball off. Most players were ready to collapse after an hour. Peter nodded at me in approval. I sensed I had had the job even before I stepped onto the court.

"We can pay $700 a month and get you a job teaching."

"I don't know. Can I have some time to think?" I said. Why play basketball here? What tempted me was the baker on the corner, the roly-poly pub owner, the friendly teammates, and the stern faced manager. And the trees.

For a few days, I lived in the Hansel and Gretel fairyland, where I expected to see breadcrumbs dropped on the cobblestone streets lined with half-timber gabled houses. I bought Mom a Hummel figurine, tucking it in my pocket and hoping that, like my heart, it wouldn't break before I got home.

I slept on a hard bed in a hotel in the town square, which dated from the 15ᵗʰ century. Breakfast was a traditional German affair: hot coffee, cold meats, a soft-boiled egg and *Brötchen* (bread rolls). Lunches and dinners, warm, robust Germans who drank beer like water surrounded me.

The day before leaving, Peter took me on a tour. From the tower, I had a breathtaking view of the villages that spilled down the green hillside into the mother tributary, Marburg. Sunlight sparkled off the emerald land.

"Marburg's one of the cleanest cities in Europe," said Peter. "It's considered the most romantic town in Germany."

I agreed. As we walked back to the car, on a trail carpeted with pine needles and lined with evergreen, I, ever passionate about the wilderness, fell in love again.

A basketball team in Geneva asked me to come to visit and to play for them. I wanted a free holiday in Switzerland at the expense of the team. Instead, I got an air mattress on the floor of an 8-by-10 foot flat and a job offer at McDonald's. One practice with this team assured me I did not want to flip burgers just to play ball at the foot of the mountains.

On the way back to Paris, I felt overwhelmed by emotions and impressions after a year abroad. I wanted to go home, but feared I was stuck on an island of strange experience that I couldn't begin to share. What about my dark-eyed, Frenchman who had stolen my heart, keeping me here, abroad with his intrigue? I longed to retreat to my beloved Summit Lake to sort out my feelings and to return to Sterling with the familiar landscape of cornfields and Midwestern voices. I worried that even at home no one would understand me. After the trauma, I needed to return to that piggy bank of my past where I could withdraw funds from my limitless family account. When I was stable, I would depart on a new adventure.

A part of me knew it was time to hang up the high tops and get a real job and I had my dad mail out my resume for coaching assistant positions at universities across the states. Was I ready to give up playing to help other athletes achieve a goal that was just out of my own reach?

Chapter 10: Fairytale Team

Germany 1981

The national federations govern the club systems with teams for children as well as senior citizens well into their sixties. Unlike the United States, anyone, male or female, at any age or skill level can participate. I envisioned myself one day, tying my gray hair into a ponytail, wearing support hose under my uniform, and hobbling down the court in Germany. Go, Granny, go.

When I flew back across the Atlantic, I thought I would leave my problems behind, but they followed me home. As usual, every summer, Phil became my sounding board. Following my dad's wishes that I stay in the States, I flew to California, interviewed for an assistantship at College of the Pacific and landed the job. With a heavy heart, I wrote Peter and told him I couldn't come to Germany. Every time the coach in California sent a packet of coaching material, my stomach turned. I loved the movement, the camaraderie, the physical aspect of the game, but never felt driven to study game strategy. I only wanted to play and dreamed of my fairytale town. At Phil's house, I paced and ranted. I threw my shoe across the room and screamed, "It's my life. I want to play."

"Then play," he said.

"But how can I go against my dad?"

"It's hard now. But you will never be happy unless you live your own life."

After a week of sleepless nights, I called College of the Pacific and explained to the coach that I still wanted to play. Then I called Peter and told him I changed my mind. Only after I finalized my decision did I tell my dad.

We were sitting on the front steps when I broke the news. Even though the sun had set, the hot, humid air sucked my breath away. The katydids' urgent cry sounded liked a siren signaling summer's end. Time had run out. The cement warmed the back of my legs, and my fingers felt clammy. The decision was killing me, but I felt like a murderess when I announced, "I'm going to Germany to play." The color drained from my father's face; he stared at me dumbfounded.

"What about your coaching contract?" he asked.

"I got out of it," I answered staring at my shoelaces. I was dressed in shorts, T-shirt and high-tops, always ready for a game.

"You were going to stay in the States — closer to home."

"California is not that close."

"You could get a plane to Chicago and be back in an emergency. In Paris, you didn't even have a phone," he said. As he pushed his glasses up onto the bridge of his nose, his hand trembled. "Why go back after all you went through in France? When you got adjusted, they sent you home."

"That had nothing to do with me," I said. "The French Basketball Federation banned foreigners."

"What if it doesn't work out?" Dad asked. "Your team in the States folded. Why do you keep trying to do this?"

One by one my dad rattled off logical arguments as to why I should quit playing professional basketball. He was right. I would never make money, nor have any job security.

"What about your back?" he asked, looking distressed.

My back. I squeezed my eyes shut and saw my crippled body strapped to a white hospital bed. My mind echoed Dad, "No, no, no," but my heart spoke louder, "Go, go, go."

"When are you going to get a real job?"

"Dad, I'm only 24. I can always get a nine-to-five. How many other chances will I have to play the game I love? To live in a new country, meet new people?"

"It makes no sense. You had a good job. A future..."

I looked at the heavens in despair wishing God had sketched the answer across the sky. All I had was an irrational, gut feeling. An act of blind faith, a spiritual calling, a destiny.

"Dad, I can't explain. I just have to go."

My father stood up, shook his head and walked into the house. The screen door slammed shut. I sat alone on the front steps of childhood, locked in my silly dreams.

Though my dad was the first to disagree with my decision to return to Europe, he was also the first to help me to prepare for another season. While the August sun scorched the cornfields, I shot baskets and my dad rebounded in a musty field house as stifling as a sauna.

I shot; he rebounded. Between the swish of the net, high tops squeaked across the floor, as I moved into position.

"Square up your feet," Dad said, "Tuck your elbow in. Snap your wrist."

I'd been raised on shooting tips, part of our ritual that started from the Sunday, fun day when I followed my dad around the gym as a child. Neither of us imagined, back then, where the game would take me.

"Concentrate. Go until you're tired, then stop," my dad said. "Too many kids ruin good form by practicing half-heartedly and throwing garbage half-court shots."

Self-discipline was deeply ingrained. My grandpa was famous for the work ethic he instilled in his former players. However, he demanded no more from his players than he expected from himself.

"Coach Mac was a living legend," President Reagan said in 1984 when he presented my grandpa with the most prestigious athletic honor, the Washington D.C. Touchdown Club Timmie Award. "Eureka still has the framed headline of a Peoria newspaper: "McKinzie Scores 52, Bradley University 0." Mac made every touchdown, every field goal, and every extra point."

Reagan's enduring admiration and affection for his former coach was typical of athletes who played for Grandpa. My grandpa's fighting spirit shaped my life and helped me to recover from major injuries to continue ball playing. His never-give-up philosophy left a lasting impression on his players because he was a living testimony of his beliefs. Grandpa just never quit. Even though he officially retired from coaching at Northern Illinois in 1962, three decades later, Grandpa, in his 90s (the oldest coach in the nation and known as the George Burns of football), was still telling the wide receivers at Eureka College how to hang onto the ball.

"Sure we had a chair for him at practice, but he never used it," Eureka's head football coach, Warner McCollum said. "Anybody who doubts he can still coach should hear one of his inspirational talks. He starts out slow, and then lets the tempo pick up. By the time he was finished, he was ready to play himself. Some of those kids cried in the dressing room."

"Walk it off," and "keep hustling" became life mottoes passed down from my athletically inclined ancestors.

While other players took time off to goof off, I tried to make up for my lack of size and physical strength with good technique developed through long hours of practice.

My dad opened the high school gym whenever he had time. He stood off to the side in his khaki pants and gray T-shirt with his arms folded across his chest, under the blue letters printed Sterling Phys. Ed. Instructor. He watched while I dribbled the length of the floor, shot lay ups and knocked down jumpers from the baseline, wing, and top of the key. He tossed balls off the backboard and I rebounded and shot them back in using both the right then the left hand. "Use your legs, cock your wrist. Get the ball in your fingertips." Dad's voice was gentle, not gruff like my grandpa's. My dad never had to yell when he was coaching me. My drive was inborn. I worked hard even when no one was watching.

Ironically, it was my dad's dedicated coaching that turned me into a pure shooter and took me far from home in pursuit of a professional basketball career. The separation was hardest on my dad. My dad would have preferred that I lived closer to home. From a father's perspective, the separation was heartbreaking, but from a coach's perspective, my success was heartwarming. My dad was the first to recognize my accomplishments and understand how much it meant to me to continue playing the game I loved.

Instinctively, my mom knew that from the time I could tie my own shoes, I was footloose and fancyfree and the world belonged to me. In 1981 my mom was miraculously reunited with my Norwegian relatives. When my grandfather's brother died, my Great Aunt Borghild Vassvic, helped by the Salvation Army, located the Olson family. Ever so honest, she wanted to assure that Gustav's family in America received their share of the small inheritance. Borghild made the connection, and treasured letters were exchanged, but my mom credited me with reuniting the families.

"Pat, if you were courageous enough to go to Paris alone," Mom told me. "Then one day I could be brave enough to fly to Evenskjer to see my family."

However at the end of the summer, no one had dry eyes, when parents drove me to the airport and sent me off with emotion-packed farewell.

My plane refueled in Iceland, then landed in Luxembourg, even though my destination was Marburg, an hour north of Frankfurt. Cheap flights never ran a straight course. At customs, my stomach knotted up with that what-if-no-one-was-here-to-meet-me déjà vu feeling? At the checkpoint, I tried to appear inconspicuous, but my oversized guitar box looked suspicious. A gruff agent yelled, *"Halt macht das ofen, bitte."* (Stop. Open this.)

"It's just a guitar," I said and began a rock 'n roll pantomime to make him understand.

Aggravated by my antics, he shook his head, pulled out a knife and cut open the box. I watched my clothes spill onto the inspection table, while an anxious line of foreigners swore in a multitude of languages at the delay. "Oh jeez," I thought. "He thinks I'm smuggling drugs."

When the customs official slashed the white athletic tape binding the black guitar case, bikini underwear popped out from under the guitar strings. Weary travelers laughed, as a red-faced agent waved me past.

I scooped my belongings into my arms and stepped through the gate scanning the crowd for a familiar face. Three Germans, looking like college students, stepped forward, calling, "Potreezia." We squeezed into the compact car between three teammates, two suitcases and a guitar, began our drive to my new home. In the backseat, I babbled to Babetta, a cute, curly-haired, brunette point guard, everyone affectionately called Bette.

"Was ist das?" I asked pointing out the window. My German vocabulary was limited to those three words.

"Castle. House. Farm," Bette repeated in English.

"No, no," I insisted. "How do you say it in German?"

My first German lesson began as a word game.

When we arrived in Marburg, we drove straight to the tennis club where a team dinner, held in my honor, had started with the first round of beer. Delirious from the excitement of travel and lack of sleep, I smiled at my new family, dozens of men and women who shared a common bond, a love for the round ball and the hard court. Then they took me to one couple's house, both basketball players, and I fell asleep as soon as my head hit the pillow on the spare cot in the hallway.

I assumed Marburg was about the size of Sterling, but when a rooster woke me up the next day, I thought I was in a village. I was wrong. Marburg blended the old—farms, half gabled houses—with the new—fast food stands, department stores, supermarkets—in a growing city of 70,000.

Every morning my host set out coffee, breads, and a soft-boiled egg before she left for work. During breakfast, Bette popped in and over coffee we'd discuss what to see that day.

As we toured the town, we looked like Mutt and Jeff, the tall, wiry American and short, sturdy German. Nestled in the Lahnberger hills, Marburg resembled a giant layer cake topped with a 13th century castle. Narrow cobblestone streets lined with stylistic burgher houses half-timbered in green, red, and gold merged at the Gothic town hall of the 10th century Old Town, where a giant cuckoo clock chimed every hour.

We walked our bikes across a footbridge to the Phillips-Universität, the oldest university in the world founded as a Protestant institution in 1527. While Bette spoke with friends, I watched the jeans-clad, German co-eds sip coffee and tea on a campus so beautiful that concentrating must have been difficult. The Lahn River traced a pale blue line through the evergreen valley where swans grazed under willow trees.

"It's gorgeous here," I said. "So clean."

"There's no industry," Bette explained, "no money either. Marburg depends on the university for income. There's a little farming: potatoes, beets, wheat, apples, and trees. It's the home of the *Tannenbaum*. And tourism, but we keep that secret."

In the whirlwind of dinners and parties that followed my first few days in a new land, I tasted the specialties of the region of Hessen, central department of Germany covering 10 percent of the country. I turned up my nose at the strong cheese, *Handkäse*, and disliked the spicy taste of *Leberkäse* sausage. The *Apfelwein* was too tangy, the *Marburger* beer too bitter. I grimaced after one sip and Bette threw her head back, laughing and said, "Don't worry, nobody here drinks it."

Even though the language and customs were foreign, I felt at home in the gym. In no time at all, my teammates were affectionately calling me Pet; the German "a" sounded like our "e." Nowhere in the world had I found such a large group that shared my love for the game. Like other European countries there were no school teams, but rather, city clubs with dozens of different boys' or girls' teams.

Even in France where the image of French femme fatale and male Don Juan reigned, women's team sports were much more socially acceptable. This was, in part, because women's teams had been established much earlier. The International Basketball Federation (FIBA) started a quadrennial World Championship for Women in 1953 (three years after that for men).

The European club system, differing from our school and professional teams, emphasized belonging to an athletic group for social reasons. In Europe, city clubs are funded by their municipalities and sponsored by businesses. Members competed according to their age and ability. From September to April, clubs practiced several nights a week and played every weekend against teams in the same division. My team played in the Bundesliga (1st division) and was composed of players from ages 18 to 32. Clubs existed for children as young as eight and for adults over age fifty. Unlike the United States where after high school or college, players must hang up their high tops, many of my old teammates, in their 30s and 40s, still enjoyed their weekly game even to this day.

Like in France, the emphasis was social rather than competitive. Equally important as the game itself was the team building meeting at the corner pub for a drink afterwards.

My transition to Germany was easier. I'd adjusted to Europe, accepting the ritual of a five-course meal in France, tolerating champagne in the locker room and refraining from smacking teammates who smoked at half time. I was also used to improvisation. If the gym was closed, we played outdoors. If the coach lacked innovative drills to develop technique, the old stand-behind-a-chair-and-shoot drill prevailed. If leather balls were unavailable, rubber would suffice. Hotel too expensive? A bunkroom will do. I didn't care what I ate, where I slept, under what conditions I played, just that I could participate.

When I arrived in Germany and discovered wooden floors were rare, drinking fountains nonexistent, new uniforms out of the question, I wasn't too concerned; but when they confessed there was no coach, I grew uneasy. They put off starting the real basketball season by having us do conditioning training. In an *eins, zwei* military style we ran across the soccer field and up and down the stadium stairs. This would have gone on indefinitely until one day when rain forced us into the gym. Peter pulled me aside and said, "You make practice."

"Okay," I said continuing shooting, "I always practice."

"No, Petreezia," he pleaded. "You trainer. You coach."

"Me?" I looked incredulous. "I don't speak German."

"It no matter. You speak basketball."

Using a coach's greatest improvising technique (when in doubt run 'em) I put my fingers to my mouth, whistled and yelled, "Line up on the end line."

With a lot of pantomime, a great deal of drama and a few keys phrases like *spitze* (great) and *scheisse* (sh**), I directed practice. Afterwards, Bette and our center, a robust, round-faced, 30-year-old, insisted on showing me their old "system." They gave me a piece of paper with lines going every which way.

"When she goes here, then she goes there, or sometimes here or she can stay there, but she'll always end up here."

Not understanding, but trying to be diplomatic, I said, "*Das ist gut*, but where's the ball?" They looked at each other befuddled, studied the scrawling and then announced triumphantly, "In the basket."

Like my grandpa, who started his coaching career in 1921 when Eureka College asked its star fullback to be head football coach two years before he graduated, I became a player/coach.

After weeks during which our mysterious coach still hadn't shown up for practice, I asked how soon he'd arrive.

"We don't know," Peter said. "He's in Turkey."

"When does he get back from vacation?"

"No vacation, he lives there."

What was a German team doing with a Turkish coach? All European teams hire players and coaches, sight unseen, based on statistics that they can't interpret because they aren't sure of the caliber of the league.

Turkey was a former colony of Germany, so many Turks immigrated to Germany. But why they would import a Turkish coach was beyond me.

While waiting for the trainer billed as the greatest basketball coach in Turkey to arrive in Germany, I organized practice for the team, no, actually, for the town. I tried to coordinate a club made up of all different ages and skill levels.

The older players were tired from working full-time and tended to sit down at practice or to not show up at all. The majority of the girls were students in their early 20s. Skill level varied greatly between the starting five and the rest, but no matter how many years of experience, no one understood simple basics like getting the ball in the middle on the fast break and blocking out to rebound on the boards.

When I was about to give up, a woman in her 30s came up to me and asked if she could play. "I work and have kids. Every year I say I retire, then start again. It must be a sickness."

I laughed. I was afflicted with the same disease. So I tried to instill the American spirit, having first to teach before I could coach, struggling to express myself with a two-year-olds' vocabulary, *ja, nein, bitte.* Why was I trying to learn another language, to adopt another culture? I knew of nowhere else in the world where Friday night entertainment was an open gym. Women didn't sit on the sidelines watching, they played alongside the men. Afterwards everyone met at the pub where the conversation was never about Barbie's divorce and Ken's affair. Everyone was discussing how Helga hit Hansel on the fast break to score the winning basket.

In the States, I begged to be allowed into pick up games with even poor ball players, but here the men's teams invited me to play in their practices insisting that I made them work harder. Afterwards, they asked me for shooting tips. For the first time, male athletes welcomed me into their inner circle. The boys I grew up with, threatened by my athletic prowess, acted wary. In Germany, men treated me like a goddess of the court.

The lack of organization annoyed me, but it seemed less important now that I was being treated as an equal. Though the competition level and quality of the facilities were better in the States, sports in Europe had something special that was often missing in America. Here basketball wasn't a game to be won or lost; it was a way of life to be lived. And everyone, young, old, fat, skinny, male, female, could play.

In Paris, I had been isolated; in Marburg there was too much social life — birthdays, carnivals, weddings. At my first birthday party, I was disappointed: we drank the cake — a keg of beer. The favorite was a plate of meat garnished with onions. I spread a generous helping on bread and then gagged on the raw hamburger. I snuck out, slipped my burger to a dog and reentered with a German shepherd at my heels.

German social life was fascinating, but frustrating because it distracted me from the task at hand. What about basketball? Basketball was not an all or nothing endeavor. It was an outlet, one of many others, something to be squeezed into a busy day for physical well-being. I, however, scheduled my life around practice, making sure I was well-rested before each session, but those sessions didn't require much rest. If I hadn't been training twice a week with the men's team, I would have been grossly out of shape.

My hosts treated me like family, but I felt like an intruder sleeping in the hallway. When I asked Peter about moving to my own apartment, he suggested I move to Bette's apartment complex on Stauffenbergstrasse where a dozen six story, low-rent, dirt brown apartment buildings perched on a steep hill at the southwestern side of town near the army base and forest. My new room was a mat on the floor of the dining room of Bette's apartment shared by five students and a dog.

I thought my other problem, coaching the team, was solved when Meshmit, returned; however, instead of striding into the gym, our short, balding, beer-bellied Turkish coach waddled into practice wearing a pair of cotton sweats that looked like pajamas and a pair of tennis shoes like house slippers. In our first drill, called airplane, we flew around the gym with our arms extended out like wings, while our all-star coach stood on the sidelines puttering, "zoom, zoom, zoom." And giggling! I'd never heard an American coach laugh in practice. In the States, basketball was business, not a comedy show. Even Meshmit's game plan was humorous. He taught us "systems" that broke all basketball rules, like setting double picks inside the lane, so we'd all get called for three-second violations.

He took out a playbook in which he had designed triangles and circles going every which way. He was writing a basketball "text" book. I took one look at it and thought, "send him back to graphic arts." If there was any logic to his drawing, only an engineer could understand it.

When we left for our first tournament, no one wished me luck; instead, the parting call was, "have fun." Like the "Bad News Bears" seven assorted-sized girls and a coach piled into a 1963 van and drove 90 mph north toward Hamburg.

"How much farther?" I asked, feeling queasy.

"Only 500 kilometers," said Bette, offering me eraser-like candy to calm my stomach. Along the way we stopped at different cities to pick up other players.

We rolled through the hills of southern Germany toward the flatlands of the north. Instead of McDonald's, bratwurst buses lined the waysides. We stopped at a roadside café, but no one could afford a $5 cheese sandwich. We saved our money for essentials: restrooms, which were 20 pfennigs, plus 10 for paper, tip not included. Now I understood why during my first road trip in France, we stopped in the country and men ran over to one side of the road and women to the other.

Finally we arrived in Hamburg, the largest harbor in Germany. The gym had the usual linoleum floor instead of wood. Before tip off, Meshmit called us to the sideline flipped five marks on the floor and showed us the system. I expected him to ask us to put our feet in the circle so he could choose the starting line up — eenie, meenie, miny, moe.

I started the game at the foul line; instead of the clamor of a crowd, I heard my stomach growling. French devour 5-course meals before the games; Germans eat Haribo's Gummi Bears.

The caliber of the game was like a pick-up game in which I played all positions. If our opponents pressed, I brought the ball up the court then passed to Bette. I'd then set up at low post, cut high, receive the pass and shoot or dish off to a teammate who was open when I drew the defense. Down by a basket, Meshmit called time-out and gave instructions in German in his singsong voice.

"What did he say?" I asked Bette.

"We have to run faster," she interpreted for me.

"That's it?" I asked shaking my head in disbelief.

"No, he also said to jump higher."

I went back to the court chuckling. I had to laugh or I'd cry. When the whistle blew again, I sat down on the bench and thought, "great, I can catch my breath before second half."

"*Schade* (too bad)," the coach repeated. "*Schade.*"

"What's too bad?" I asked Bette.

"Too bad we lost," she answered.

I stared at the clock. "Isn't it half-time?"

After the game, Meshmit explained special tournament rules, two 12 (instead of 20) minute halves.

In the next game, I was so mad I scored 30 points in the first half. Still losing in the second half, in my over-zealous attempt to ensure victory, I fouled out in a rare feat — four charging fouls. I complained as my teammates ushered me to the sideline and explained another tournament rule, four (not five) fouls and you're out. I sat on the sideline nursing a black eye, bloody lip, and broken heart, wondering what every benched player wonders — where'd the referee lose his glasses? In the middle of a fast break, a teammate hobbled over to the sideline. The play would have continued four against five until I nudged Bette and told her to get in the game. I checked the books, but the only statistics recorded were baskets made and at which they minute were scored.

"What about the game stats? You know, rebounds, turnovers, recoveries, assists?" I asked a teammate.

"What do mean turnover, recovery, assist?"

I walked to the end of the gym taking deep breaths. Do not take yourself too seriously. Remember this is only a game. My older brother's advice came back to haunt me. "Don't worry about basketball. You might not learn a thing about the game, but with Europe as a playground, you'll learn about people."

After my first year abroad, I learned to keep basketball in perspective, but it did not come naturally because for so many years, I lived and died every game. The daughter of a state championship high school coach and the granddaughter of a seven-time Hall of Fame college coach meant that the competitive spirit was ingrained. In a sense I had to unlearn everything I had believed to be true about sports. Winning was not everything, but being on the court was. No longer allowed to play in my own country, I kept reminding myself that I was lucky to be in a land where I was welcome in the game.

My teammates with culturally entrenched attitudes different from my own, understood far better than I that basketball was a small part of life involving other things to see and do. That night we strolled down the wide, neon-lit streets of downtown Hamburg and ate the universal pizza. Unlike in the U.S. where we were paid to play (in theory) and in France where a sponsor paid, here we picked up our own tabs.

After dinner I was ready to sleep, but I soon learned that the "fun" was just beginning. We returned to our "Hyatt Regency," an old schoolhouse. I curled up in a sleeping bag and retreated to the corner. Within minutes the rival teams burst into the room and began passing around cheap Italian champagne, Sekt. The slumber-less party began. At 8:00 a.m. we rolled up the gym mats from under our sleeping bags and got out the basketballs. During the warm-ups, our opponents passed around coffee and the hard rolls. Then the players struggled up and down the court, finishing the tournament.

When we arrived home feeling wearier from the festivities than from the game itself, our friends met us at our favorite pub to hear about the trip. Naturally, the first question they asked me was, "Did you have fun?"

"Fun? *Ja, Ja,*" I said and added with a spirit only another American could appreciate, "It was fun, we won!"

I'd been living in Marburg two months when I finally got a

room of my own. Our center, Britt, a large-boned, blonde, had the middle room that served as a living room. Anja, a guard, lived in the room at the end of the hall. We shared a kitchen nook that was the size of an American bathroom. My room, inside the door across from the bathroom, was furnished with hand-me-downs from the community. My single bed had a two-inch thick mattress filled with straw. A straight back chair sat at a desk overlooking the valley and an armoire with a broken leg perched precariously in one corner. When visitors came, I dragged in chairs from our kitchen or we sat on the floor around a teakettle warmed over a candle flame.

Other teammates, housed in the same complex, were students, too. Like living in a commune, we shared clothes, food, and chores, like mopping the communal apartment steps. Bette let everyone borrow her car. Though we were all pacifists, we called ourselves the Stauffenbergstrasse Mafia.

Our days, especially weekends, began with *Frühstuck*, the traditional German breakfast of hot coffee, bread, homemade jellies, meats, and cheeses. We talked for hours. By reading facial expressions and gestures, I learned the language, if not well enough to speak fluently, then at least to comprehend.

"*Du bist so din*," my teammates lamented that I was too thin.

I was underweight compared to the Germans. My build, like the French, was slender and angular, not robust and sturdy. In France I felt too tall; in Germany, I felt too thin.

When my teammates left for class, I borrowed Bette's typewriter and pecked my way through articles cursing the German keyboard for sticking a "z" where the "a" should be. Our city newspaper's editor asked me to be a correspondent. Though I'd never written for publication, I drew a following because everyone in town knew me as a hoop star. Initially my writing rambled, but the topic, life abroad, captivated the locals as they lived vicariously through my travels.

I craved new experiences as much as basketball, for more stories to tell. It was more important to play, to actively participate, than to win. So I chased a silly game, in search of a place where I could become a part of something bigger than myself. As an outsider I stepped back from events, seeing as from a bystander's perspective. I searched for a niche where the onlooker and the participant could be as one. I found this oneness on the court. After the exhilaration of the game, was the relaxing euphoria of a steamy locker room, followed by a cold pint at the pub. I clung to my constant—basketball, thriving on sweat and living out my hard court dreams.

"I am a stranger in my birthplace; at home in a foreign country, forever alone, yet always a part of mankind."

I filled my journals with the soul-searching one does after moving to a foreign country and dropping into non-existence until another identity is forged.

At times I felt homesick, but where was home? Letters kept me longing for Paris and Gérald. I missed my family in America, but I felt so welcome with teammates in Germany.

The nights were long, but the days flew by. The only time I sat still was when I was writing in the mornings. Then I hopped on my bike and coasted down our mountain, to my orthopedic doctor. There I'd peel out of sweaters a size too big and jeans a size too small, as was fashionable, for my heat treatment and back massage. The German fee was reimbursed by state-funded insurance. My only insurance was a winning season; the doctor, an avid fan, treated me for free.

In the afternoon, I pedaled my bike down the cobblestone streets of old town towards the American House library. I read, taking time out for an afternoon cup of tea. Seventy-five cents, the price of a hot drink, afforded me a table where I could linger over a cup all day filling notebooks with impressions.

At dusk, my day really began. Every night I attended adult education classes. One evening, I studied French, struggling to grasp the German interpretation; another night I took German, equally befuddled. On my favorite night, my guitar replaced my book bag and I strummed along with Hubertus, chanting *Deutsch* to old American folk tunes.

But most evenings I spent at home, home being *Grossportfield* gym. During the normal American dinner hour, I fed my kids fundamentals. My job was teaching 10-year-old boys how to play basketball. After an hour and a half with twenty kids, I collapsed on the bench, but one of the guys pulled me to my feet and begged me to practice with the men's team. At 8:30 p.m., my teammates danced in with my tape player, sharing my addiction to music. Practice started with a leisurely game of tag and ended with a laborious scrimmage against the men. We finished the evening in the corner pub. I sipped *Sprudel*, carbonated water, while friends gulped beer. My education began in the pubs. Teammates debated political theories, world events, and social issues. One night they discussed German history and the Nazi rise to power. Teammates expressed profound shame about the concentration camps.

"To this day, we are embarrassed about this part of our heritage," Anja said. "Our parents can remember the Hitler youth camps and how he took over the socialization process. My dad told me it was as if the German people no longer had a mind of their own. Today, the older generation wants to not think about it, so it is never discussed."

Most of my teammates were educated college students working toward degrees in teaching, psychology or medicine, so I often times struggled to follow the intellectual discussions held in a foreign tongue.

The only thing missing from my life was a job. Peter promised me one along with my salary, a flat, and a car. I arrived in Marburg to a warm welcome, but no car, no apartment, and no work; instead I was given a bicycle, a basketball, and a beer and told, *"Kein problem"* (no problem.) The lack of employment bothered me the most. Playing ball for a living was too easy to be considered work. My teaching job fell through. A player on the men's team worked in a gym. I asked if I could share the responsibilities handing out equipment, but the janitor said, "I'll never work with a nigger or a woman." Peter reassured me that coaching kids was enough, but I wanted to contribute more to the community.

In Germany, the club manager agreed to pay me $700 a month. We shook on it. Every month, I had no idea where the money came from, but the agreed-upon amount was in the bank. In France, I received a manila envelope once a month containing the 5.000 French Francs that I hid in a shoebox under my bed. When I played in the WBL, we had business managers and coaches from the NBA. We met with lawyers and signed contracts, but never got paid a dime. I figured one man's word was as good as his signature. Playing in Germany was so simple, it was like taking candy from a baby. But no one got rich shooting hoops, at least not in the women's league in the early '80s. In Europe, only the men's first division teams could entice players with six figure salaries. In the women's league, few players other than foreigners were paid. Most German women paid for their players' license and travel expenses. The community played a benevolent role. Locals volunteered to be club administrators, donating their time and furnishing meals. But no separation between the administration and the team existed. They were often one and the same. Consequently, the people making decisions concerning the team were often the least knowledgeable about the game. It was as logical as a basketball coach walking into Maxim's in Paris and telling the French chefs how to cook.

One night they called a club meeting. Peter discouraged me from attending, but everyone else was going so I thought it must be important. City Hall was filled with fifty people lining wooden tables headed by the club president, a banker, to discuss the financial problems. The club, sponsored only by private contributors, was going broke. They could never pay three Americans, the boy's foreign player, a coach, and me.

"We'll have to send someone home," the president said.

"Not Pet," Peter said. "The girls are in first division. It's a good team. Cut the men's budget, they're in third division."

"We aren't sending anybody home," said the manager of the men's team. "They need jobs. The guys work outside the club. What does Pet do?"

"She coaches the *kinder*," Peter said defending me.

"She doesn't have an apartment like the guys," Anja said. "She lives with us; we pay our own rent."

I looked around the room at all the players who treated me like a sister, and felt sick. I thought we were family.

"We should invest in the women's program. They have a better team," said one of the men's players. "More money should go to them; they get all the fans."

"Then we cut the men's budget."

"It's not fair. We contribute outside incomes."

My hand shook as I raised it. In faulty German, I addressed the community. "I asked for a job. I want to work, to help the club. They told me there are no jobs. I have no work papers."

Peter's face crumbled as though I'd stabbed him. Board members looked down at their notes, unable to meet my eye. Both male and female friends' lips curved into knowing smiles.

My voice cracked, but I continued, "Why bring us here if you don't want us to stay? Why not figure your budget before the season started? I don't want to leave," I blurted. I stumbled as I pushed my chair from the table and ducked into the night.

As I trudged up the Tannenberg hill, I looked at the starlit sky and prayed, hoping I wasn't being selfish in my demands.

"Please, just one more season!"

Chapter 11: Bratwursts, Beer and Basketball

Marburg Germany 1981-82

"Federation de Basketball Amateur (FIBA)
founded in Geneva, Switzerland in 1932
governs over 450 million players and 213
federations in 2006."
-FIBA Website http://www.fiba.com

The crisp autumn air stung my hot cheeks as I trudged uphill toward my apartment. Then I heard footsteps. Bette ran up and slipped her arms around me. *"Komme* Patty. It's not important. It's the same ol' bullshit. The president always talks crap. They aren't sending anybody home, especially not you."

"I feel stupid. I shouldn't have said anything,"

"Nein, they should know how you feel. We know you want a job. You came to help, not to live off of us. You are different from the rest."

Ah, yes, the image of the Ugly American. Many of my male counterparts who came to play in the European league never tried to learn a word of French, German, or Italian. They only wanted to make as much money as possible and then go back.

"Komme. Du muss das vergessen."

But I couldn't forget, it was so important to be part of a community. When my roommates came home, they consoled me by telling me what had been decided at the meeting concerned only the finances of the men's team, not ours.

"We want you to be happy here," the board members' wives said when they came by with gifts and apologies the next day.

"But I am," I said as my face turned crimson and cold sweat rolled down my inner arm. *"Ich mag ganz Marburg und alle die Leute."*(I like Marburg and all the people.)

In a strange twist of fate, I, a woman, was paid more than the men and was on a better team with a bigger public drawing. For the first time, I did not have to settle for being second to the men's program. Instead of feeling pride, I felt guilty and feared that one of the guys would be sent home because of me.

After sitting on the sideline, I was finally allowed to play, but only for a limited time under the worst conditions, even though I attended one of the best women's basketball colleges.

Though the Title IX law mandated equal opportunity in state-funded schools and universities, things had not yet been equal. It wasn't fair, but I never got militant. Instead of carrying signs, burning bras, and becoming vocal, I fought the battle in silence, proving by my actions, by the way I played ball—my skill level, my intensity, my determination—that I was equal.

Now on this German team, I, the woman, was being made the priority as the men's team took the back seat to our program. On the one hand I felt relieved, but on the other, uncomfortable. I empathized with the other half. I knew how bad it felt to lack financial support. Rather than rejoicing in my hard fought victory, I felt ill at ease. My struggle for equal rights was a fight for women, not a battle against men. Downtrodden for so many years, I felt undeserving of the privileged treatment. Despite my parents' efforts, my coaches' efforts, and my own efforts to prove otherwise, as a girl who was raised in America in the '70s, I was socialized to believe I was second best. A decade later in another land, with the tables turned, instead of feeling exultant, as I should, I felt ashamed. But not for long because my next road trip was to Munich!

The best part about playing basketball in Europe was the travel. I was so excited the night before our trip to Munich that I couldn't sleep. A few weeks after our Turkish coach's arrival, and filled with confidence knowing that the club guaranteed my job, at least for this year, I led a team strike refusing to play for Meshmit, so we got a new coach, Hans Brauer, who was a physical education teacher and player for the men's team. Like my French coach, my new German coach was lovable. Later he would marry one of my teammates and go on to become a successful coach in Germany. Their daughter, Jenny, would make her mark in basketball, too. However back then, whatever he lacked in game strategy as a first time coach, he made up for with an uncanny understanding of women. Surprisingly, we remained in first place until we met Munich, the powerhouse of Germany.

Our league consisted of 12 teams that played 11 home and away games. Teams were ranked by a point system in which a victory was one point and a tie was a half a point. The four top teams had a playoff at the end of the season. My German coach, like my French coach, calculated which games we could win. Munich was not one of them, so he approached the weekend in Munich as a fun outing, not an important game.

I felt like I'd walked into Disneyland when I stepped into Munich's Marienplatz, the spiral-towered town square. We munched on pie-sized pretzels while watching the carillon's 140-meter-high copper figures pop out of the tower in the Gothic Town Hall and perform a dance commemorating the wedding of Bavarian Duke Wilhelm V to Dutchess Renata Lothringen.

Part of the reason the local girls played on club teams was for the experiences travel brought. That night we dined on regional specialties: *Schweinhacks,* roasted pig thigh, and hand-packed potato balls. Then we went to the *Hofbrauhaus,* founded in 1589 by Duke Wilhem V to supply the court with beer. We sat at a long wooden banquet table amidst a hodge-podge of languages. My teammates insisted I drink a beer. Just one. A buxom blond Bavarian woman, spilling out of her laced green and white bodice served me a glass, a *Mass* about the equivalent of one quart. While brass bands boomed, we swayed arm and arm and sipped our never-ending beer.

The next day, I was the only one who was nervous before the game. "Relax, Pat," Bette whispered before tip-off. "This game doesn't matter, and we can't win."

Like most American athletes, I refused to accept anything less than victory, so I tried my best. The after-effect of our night out and one giant beer ruined my concentration. I fouled a girl and she went to the line for the free throw. I stood under the basket, knees flexed, anticipating the rebound. When the ball hit the rim and bounced off, I jumped, caught the ball in the air and shot it back off the bank board. It swished around the net and dropped in. The crowd burst out laughing. My face burned as I fell to my knees and pounded the floor. I made history as the first American star to score a basket for the opponent.

My teammates would never let me forget. On Saint Nicholas night, December 6th, at our team's Christmas party, Peter dressed as a red-robed Saint Nick. One of the younger boys, disguised as Ruprecht or Hans Muff, was at his side carrying a bag of gifts for the good and twigs for the bad.

When Saint Nick called, "Petreezia," I stepped forward into a circle of teammates. *"Ich war ein gutes Madchen,"* I boasted.

"*Ja, Ja.* You were good girl. You only made one mistake, but we have something here to help you with directions," Saint Nick said, as he handed me a cardboard basketball court with a compass in the middle. The room rocked with laughter.

"But we love your spirit," he said as he gave me a musical gingerbread house made from the German Christmas specialty "*Lebkuchen*" that played our warm-up songs.

After each player received his gag gift from Saint Nick, we exchanged presents among the teams. Someone flipped on an American cassette and we danced until dawn, then those of us left standing returned home for breakfast.

The complications of making plans for the Christmas vacation forced me to try to unify my three identities. My parents wanted to visit on the holidays and as much as I wanted to see them, I felt ashamed of my nomadic existence and wondered where they could comfortably sleep in our commune. Gérald called to invite me to spend the holiday with his family in Normandy. I was afraid to see him again; simply hearing his voice kept me awake all night. Whenever I felt homesick, I took the train to France. When I crossed the border, I left my comfy German clothes behind and became Patreesha, a French girl, in dangling earrings, dark eye make-up, and a dash of perfume to accentuate my femininity. Clad in fringed suede boots, skin tight jeans, a sweater and scarf, I couldn't let go of the French in me, the charming, coy, cunning woman, who hung on to a lover she vowed to leave.

My life in Germany was good; my only problem was self-discipline. I was happy to put aside my studies for morning breakfast, afternoon tea, and evening wine with friends. We socialized until there was nothing left to say, and then I retreated to my world of words.

I twisted and turned on my hard bed, under my heavy German quilt. I lay awake at night making up stories about the three separate lives I lived. I tried to learn German while retaining my French, but longed to be an American writer. On the side, I supported my habit—basketball. Could I have a multiple personality disorder, developing three different identities, falling in love with three different countries?

Peter and I picked up my folks at the Frankfurt airport for the holiday break. The Americans with their excess of baggage stuck out in the throng of arrivals. After hugging my parents, we whisked them off to Nuremberg for our basketball game.

We tromped through the world-famous open-air Christmas market on the cobblestone streets before heading to the gym. We should have won the game by 20, but finished just a point ahead with my final-second free throw. On the train home, my team shrugged off their poor game and celebrated by popping open Sekt. Bette aptly summarized the game, "Oh it was very hard," and I collapsed into her arms agreeing as she continued, "No, not for us, for your parents. They had to see it."

The strain of the game was a warm-up for the next grueling event—the ride home. We crowded fifteen people into a six-passenger compartment. In the midst of our party, the train bolted to a stop, we bounced off and the bewildered Americans asked, "Did we get kicked off for being too rowdy?"

"*Nein,*" said our coach, his speech slurred. "We change lines. We followed his lead to the wrong train, and then had to sprint to catch the next one. Four hours and three trains later we arrived in Marburg.

"You'll never see Marburg unless we get out of this store," I pleaded. Mom asked my friends where she could buy one of those world famous porcelain Hummel figurines. None of my Germans friends had ever heard of them. Dad insisted on buying a beer mug. "But, Dad, you don't drink beer."

"It's not to drink out of. It's to look at." *Ach,* the Germans would be appalled. Whoever heard of admiring an empty beer stein in *Deutschland*?

After a few days in Marburg, a French friend took us on a sightseeing tour of northeastern France via Neiderbreisig. "Who ever heard of Neiderbreisig?" I asked. "It's not in the Michelin guide book. It can't be famous."

"Yes, it is," Dad announced. "Grandpa was stationed there during World War I."

Grandpa never complained when his brilliant college career was interrupted by WWI. He was proud to serve in the U.S. Army. So in 1918, instead of zigzagging across a football field, he marched from Cherbourg, France, to Neiderbreisig, Germany, where he was shot by one of his own men in a freak accident. I remembered hearing my Grandpa tell the story.

"I was in charge of the rec [recreation] room. A drunk private got in a fight with the cook. Some of the guys put him to bed," recounted Grandpa. "But he came back, shot at the cook, missed, and hit me in the back. The bullet was deflected by a rib, circled my rib cage, and came out a quarter of an inch below my heart. Doctors said it was a one-in-a-million shot!"

After he recovered, Grandpa returned to Eureka, where he was named coach and athletic director of all sports while still a junior academically. He guided the Eureka football team to several championships and won three straight Little 19 Conference basketball championships. In 1937, he continued his coaching success at NIU where, as head basketball coach, he won three Interstate Conference titles in eight years. Then he gave up basketball to coach baseball, winning three more Interstate Conference titles in the next eight seasons. I revered my grandpa, so Neiderbreisig or bust!

Three hours later, after finally finding the village, which had been renamed, I insisted, "No, Dad, you can't buy any souvenirs. All the shops are closed on Christmas Eve."

"But I saw a light on in that corner store," he said. Before I could stop him, the car door slammed and he was tapping at the grocer's living room window babbling about the family history. Minutes later, my dad returned clutching a dust-covered can of sauerkraut.

In my half-sleep stupor, exhausted from interpreting, I missed the tour, but I could see it all later for every sight was captured on film — not once, but twice!

"Oh, Honey, I don't know if that picture turned out on the pocket instamatic. Better get another one on the Minolta." Two dozen rolls of film later, we returned to Marburg.

One night we had an American practice with a special guest coach, my dad. Even this 50-year-old man played and was accredited with one old-fashioned hook shot and an air ball. A teammate had a *Feuerzangenbowle* fest, which featured a special holiday brew of red wine, rum, orange juice, and spices boiled in a copper kettle. The following evening the Americans were toasted with a strong, dark, winter brew, *Buck* beer. All this drinking prepared a non-drinking, ulcer-plagued American coach for his final night in Europe, *Sylvester* (New Year's Eve.) The Americans' trip abroad ended with a bang, literally. To bring in the New Year in Germany, everyone flooded the streets, throwing firecrackers.

Before leaving the next morning, my parents emptied their suitcases, which were filled with American gifts for my teammates, and refilled them with German souvenirs. Peter drove us to the airport. When I kissed my dad, his cheek was damp with the realization that his little girl would never come home. While we waved good-bye to my parents, trailed by their family of suitcases, Peter teased me about the American preoccupation with luggage. I imagined overhearing Dad marvel to Mom about the amazing quantities of beer Germans could consume. Even after meeting face-to-face, the stereotypes of the jovial beer-loving Germans and photo-snapping Americans were still intact, but a new dimension enlightened the common misconceptions. Despite one another's amusing eccentricities, both parties would agree that those across the big blue sea really were wonderful people. As Peter drove across the snow-covered fields, I rubbed my tired eyes, feeling weary but heart-warmed from being the go-between to connect countries and cultures.

The next night as I rode my bike down the cobblestone streets, snowflakes kissed my cheeks, Christmas lights twinkled from the rooftops of the half-timbered shops, and I smiled in the afterglow of the holidays. I wore a sweater of Dad's, Sue's old boots, Karen's old jeans, Bette's flannel shirt, and Gérald's scarf while I balanced on Peter's old bike. My mismatched attire, hardly Paris fashion, warmed me from the inside out.

By the end of the week, my first snowfall euphoria disappeared. I was tired of the all-day chill and frozen nights. Robust German flat mates slept with the heat turned down and the windows open. I lay awake on my pallet of straw with my teeth chattering and my toes numb, resorting to hot baths in the middle of the night to thaw my extremities. Without the warm surge of love, I could never have survived the winter.

My friends, like most college students in their second childhood before facing real life, found excuses to throw parties: birthdays, final exams, weekends. The entire country invented reasons to celebrate, the biggest being *Fasching*, a carnival tradition dating from the 14th century. Wooden-masked marauders danced in the fields, defying local authority, to ensure a good crop. Then the public, costumed and with their faces painted, marched through the marketplace and did whatever shouldn't be done, before making the Lenten sacrifices on Ash Wednesday. Children weren't the only ones in costumes—even the adults acted like clowns. Bette dressed as a witch, her boyfriend dressed as a farmer, and I became a Native American. Arm in arm we walked down our hill, singing and sipping a *Piltz* from a brown bottle. In Old Town we joined the mass of merrymakers to watch the Rosen Montag parade. Bette's boyfriend popped the parade queen's balloon bosom, I stole a float flower, and Bette stuffed a sausage in a tuba.

Still weary from the town party, I wasn't even looking forward to my 25th birthday that a teammate, born two days before me, insisted we celebrate together in usual commune fashion with all of the first and second division men's and women's teams and other friends outside the club. I came home from a bad practice dejected, afraid I would never fit in this country, nor ever find my place in life.

The morning of my birthday, my roommates and friends shooed me out of the apartment and told me to go upstairs and chop onions for goulash soup. I sat, alone, in my neighbor's kitchen weeping from cutting onions.

Hours later, Bette came and put a blindfold over my eyes, then led me downstairs. When she took the blindfold off, I was standing in front of the clean beige walls of a new room. They put their paintbrushes down as I wrapped them in a hug. That evening, the troops filled the apartment with noise and laughter, and devoured the soup and *boule* (wine mixed with fruit). My room filled up with flowers, books, drawings, and knick-knacks of affection, simple reminders of how welcome I was in this foreign country. That night, like a princess, I fell asleep in a bed of rose petals in a fairyland of love.

The following weekend was an even greater gift: we upset Dorsten, the second-ranked team in Germany to qualify for the quarterfinals. No one had expected us to win. We were the underdogs, the Bad News Bears, a tossed together team that laughed a lot and sipped Sekt. I had waited a lifetime for this magic moment in sport, a victory won on teamwork. Dorsten had better, stronger players, but we were more united and each individual played her best. After the game, we jumped for joy in a giant team hug. Every defeat was worth this moment of triumph. Then at the tennis club, we celebrated with the men's team and our fans.

Every night when I walked down the steep hill from my apartment toward the gym, I stared at the castle glowing in the mist on the hill across town and thought how much I loved living here and how much I wanted to stay. But playing basketball was not enough. Peter promised me a job and told me that if I could pass the entrance exam, I could attend the university. I studied German in order to pass the test, so that I could enroll in English and P.E. classes in the university. Every morning, I sat in a room filled with foreigners, listening to news reports, struggling to read the paper, and worrying about passing the all-important *Prüfung* (exam). In the afternoon, I sat in a narrow train-sized café, *Die Zug*, watching the people and writing stories for the newspaper.

I listened to the news about the problems between countries in the European Economic Community (EEC) and knew that if an act so simple as ordering a meal could not be accomplished without misunderstanding, communication between the 12 different countries of the EEC must be impossible. The locals, who lined the bar, grumbled about the number of foreigners and the lack of jobs. In France, the people disliked Arab immigrant workers; Germans disfavored the Turks. My shoulders slumped as I sipped tea and felt guilt that I, too, was a foreigner who was stealing someone's job, eating some German's supper, and not putting back into the land as much as I was taking from it.

When living in France, I had often heard criticism of American politics and in Germany the situation was no different. My educated, political-conscience, leftist teammates loved to tease me about the American President, whom they called Rea Gun, so I didn't dare tell them he was a personal family friend. My grandpa even flew for the first time when Reagan invited his old coach to attend his inauguration in Washington D.C. Consequently, political conversations always made me feel uncomfortable. Though my European experiences gave me a global view and I could understand my friends' perspective, I felt like a traitor questioning my own country's foreign policies, as if I were bad-mouthing a relative.

The next day I went to see Peter about a teaching opportunity. He shook his head and said, "Sorry. It fell through. We'll find you money to stay on. Just worry about passing your test."

"But I want to earn my money."

"You do. You play great and teach children how to play."

Dejected, I returned to the gym. Before practice with the kids, a little girl handed me white flowers in a pink napkin. When I leaned down to kiss her cheek, she whispered, "*Ich liebe dich*" (I love you.) I couldn't give up. I volunteered to work with handicapped adults in addition to helping coach the wheelchair basketball team.

For our final season game we played Dorsten again in a battle for third place. A jazz band played "When the Saints Come Marching In" while we dribbled in for lay-ups at warm-ups. I heard my kids scream, *"Auf gehts* (go) Patty!" I saw members of the wheelchair basketball team that I also helped coach, fixed in place, applauding each move I made on the court. At the free throw line, I heard our fans scream and whistle. I found my home in a foreign land. Then somehow, we lost by a basket and my sense of belonging dissolved. My teammates and club members united at the tennis club for the celebration — our season was successful — all I could think about was the final score of the final game. I felt like I had let the entire team down. But as they dragged me out into town, everywhere I went people congratulated us on a great game, a fabulous season.

After our final game, instead of hopping on a plane for home, I stayed on, determined to learn the language.

One gorgeous May morning I overslept, so I hopped on my bike in a rush to get to the university for class. Apple and cherry blossoms dotted a palate of green as I coasted down Tannenberg at breakneck speed. I reached back to untangle my book bag strap, then felt my bike spin out of control, pitching me over the handlebars. I landed on my head and shoulder. My bike's bent pink frame lay another ten yards away. When I stood up, my knees buckled under me. Yellow lights flashed. I staggered back up the hill to my apartment. Bette saw me weaving through the parking lot like a drunk.

"Patty *was hat passiert?"*

"Patty what happened?" she repeated in English staring at my smashed bike. I looked at my best friend, dumbfounded, unable to speak.

"Oh no, not off our mountain, *oh mein liebe Gott,"* (my dear God) she said as she eased me into the back seat of her car. "I'm taking you to a doctor."

While Bette sped through my dream town, I held my head up in my hands and watched the pink, white, and blue houses blur into a giant pastel of colored lines, like an impressionist painting. It would be years before I saw clearly again.

The orthopedic doctor took X-rays, put me in a neck brace, and ordered bed rest. My head throbbed. The room spun. I wanted to go home where I was sure my doctor could put me back together again like Humpty Dumpty after the great fall.

My mind was a mess, too. My life was in Marburg, Germany; my love in Paris, France; my family in Sterling, Illinois, U.S.A.

I was a physical wreck, not only from the accident, but also from illness. Throughout the season I had become sick repeatedly with mononucleosis and strep throat. A doctor gave me white tablets and red syrup and ordered rest, but I kept going especially after the accident. When I slowed down, all I heard was a carpenter pounding nails in the back of my head.

I flew home to Sterling for the summer holidays, where I hoped American doctors could repair the damage.

"You see a doctor after you fell off that bike?" my chiropractor asked frowning at my X-rays. "This is a serious whiplash injury."

"They don't have chiropractors in Germany; I saw an orthopedic surgeon. He put me in a neck brace and told me I could play a sport where I wasn't using my arms."

"You shouldn't be playing anything! You've done more damage. Instead of curving back, the vertebrae in your neck curve forward," he explained showing me on the skeleton. "Anytime you run, you are pinching the nerves to your brain."

"I feel dizzy; I can't get enough oxygen to my brain."

"I'll do what I can, but no sports."

"The team wants me to come back at the end of summer."

"We'll wait. See how you respond to treatment."

"Doc, I'll do whatever you say, please, stop the pounding at the base of my skull!"

An arm went numb. One ear was plugged up. My head sat crooked on my shoulder. I lived a teeter-tottery existence. My off-balance body felt like it was falling.

More treatments. More X-rays. After weeks without change, we started traction three times a day, and no exercise. None. I hung myself three times a day—my neck hooked in a noose connected to a five-pound water bag slung over the door pulling my cervical vertebrae.

Summer days, like popsicles in the sun, melted together while I stumbled through the motions of life, wondering why no one noticed I was losing my mind. By evening I was dragged under by the tidal wave. Then the ants came marching in. The tingling numbness, like a wind out of nowhere, rustled through my hair sending chills down my spine. Light-headed, I'd lie down and close my eyes, but the room spun. Doctors discovered a nerve going into my eyes was in constant motion, which was why I felt dizzy and had the sensations of falling.

In college as my mom watched me compete on the court, she may have worried about my lean frame bashing bigger bodies in the tough league, but she never told me. As she nursed my sprained ankle, separated rib, black eye, broken finger, and another concussion, she may have shuddered inside, but I only saw the smile.

When I hit the wall diving for a loose ball, or got slammed on a rebound, she may have cringed inwardly, but outwardly she remained calm. I only heard her shout of encouragement every time I got up and back in the game.

Though her heart must have been filled with trepidation, her voice remained positive and reassuring as she drove me to Chicago for intensive eye and ear tests and a brain scan to determine the damage from my latest fall.

After the tests, the doctors told me there was no blood clot or brain damage, but then reiterated a warning I'd heard before. "If you continue playing, it's at your own risk."

Risk or die, I thought as I boarded my plane for Germany with my college teammate and best friend, Vonnie, my former college teammate at my side. "Don't worry," Vonnie assured my family as we boarded the plane, "I'll take good care of her."

Chapter 12: Miracle Ride

Germany, fall 1982, winter 1983

"Miracle – an event that appears to be contrary to the laws of nature and regarded as an act of God."

Webster's Dictionary

The stoic Deutsche Bank teller, clad in black, stood ramrod straight. His face dropped when two *Auslanders* (foreigners) in disheveled sweats and tennis shoes strode to his desk and asked to withdraw money. He scowled as he shoved forward bank statements.

"Hey, my account says zero!" Vonnie exclaimed.

"Could be worse," I said handing her my printout. "Mine is in the red!"

Then, much to the clerk's bewilderment, we laughed so hard we cried. Laugh was what we did best in those days as pioneers in professional basketball. Most of the time, blinded beyond reason and driven in pursuit of our dreams, we endured hardships and inconveniences.

Vonnie, who hailed taxis to ride two blocks to our college gym, never complained about walking to practice in Marburg. The half-timbered homes, circling the 15th century castle in the green valley that once inspired the Brothers Grimm, captured her artist's eye and my writer's mind. But when we met with our German team manager in the pub and he explained that the Bundesliga allowed only one American per team, even laid-back Vonnie looked alarmed.

"But I am an American, too!" Vonnie said.

Peter sipped his frothy beer, leaned over the heavy wooden table and whispered, *"Nein, kein Amerikannerin. Du bist Russisch."* (No American. You are Russian.)

"Did he say I'm Russian?" Vonnie asked me. "I thought we were allowed two foreigners."

"Shhshh," Peter motioned with his left forefingers to his lips, while reaching into his back pocket with his right hand.

"Two foreigners. One American," he said. Then winking at Vonnie, he slid a pocket-sized booklet towards her, *"und ein*

Russin" (and one Russian).

"That's illegal!" Vonnie said, shoving the passport back. "I'm not doing time in Russia!"

Peter pushed it back at us. Gingerly, I picked up the document and turned to the first page. We stared in disbelief. Sure enough, Vonnie Tomich had become Yvonne Varvic, born in Kiev.

Vonnie, an Orthodox Serbian American, knew a few Serbian words and all of their customs, which was our only saving grace. With her jet-black hair and eyes, she passed as Slavic, but teammates remained skeptical.

"What was it like in Russia?" Bette asked over coffee.

"I don't know," Vonnie mumbled and stuffed her mouth with a roll. "Soon as I was born, we got the hell out of there."

"No one gets out of Russia," Bette insisted, "especially during the Cold War."

"I don't know how we settled paperwork. Thank God they let us stay in the States."

During the excitement of our winning season, I forgot the passport fraud. But Vonnie spent sleepless nights obsessing about how to survive on bread and water in prison once the authorities found out she was pretending to be America's archenemy.

"What can I tell the reporters?" Vonnie lamented when the local TV scheduled a special feature about the Russian and American who starred on the German team.

"Call Peter. He got us into this. He'll get us out of it." Sure enough, the TV dropped the story; eventually our friends dropped the subject. But as we continued winning, the media returned.

The most essential thing to bring along when living abroad was a friend. For me, a shooting forward, having a best friend who was a point guard who passed you the ball was ideal. Vonnie looked out for me on and off the court and was the only one who understood the gravity of my neck injury.

She was also one of the few people like me who could live comfortably amidst chaos. For weeks she slept on her pile of belongings in the corner of my room until my roommates moved. I agreed to a cut in pay to help finance a second foreigner. Money seemed inconsequential. We had a roof overhead, food on the table, and a winning team. Like in college, Vonnie made me look good on the court. She knew where I was at all times and hit me whenever I was open.

She became my guardian angel. She loved to cook and made sure we ate a balanced diet. Without her keeping me laughing, I could not have survived the pain. Before and after every practice and game, Vonnie checked to make sure my spine was lined up straight, when I lay down on the floor in traction with my head pulled taut from a strap attached to the wall. My chiropractor in the States had sent me back abroad with a make shift traction device. Vonnie sat beside me on the floor chattering about the game, joking about the life we lived. On the court she screamed at me to stay out from under the boards and begged me to give up the baseline when a girl twice my size barreled toward the basket and me. For fleeting moments I was lost in the joy of movement; on the fast break, Vonnie hit me with a pass on the wing and I glided to the hoop. But most of the game, I played with fear, calculating every move to bring the least amount of pain. By half-time, my head felt like it had slipped off my shoulder and the fingers of my right hand were numb. For the rest of every game, I concentrated on stopping the basket from wavering long enough to take my shot. The shooting gesture ingrained from hours of practice remained consistent. I could not feel the ball on my fingertips, but I still made baskets. Even though the left side of my brain went numb, and my head throbbed and spun, on the way home from victory as our beat-up blue van bounced across the verdant hills to the tune of Diane Ross's "Upside Down," I felt high. And happy.

I believed if I could just find a chiropractor, he could put my head back on straight, with one pop, but chiropractors were rare in Germany. My chiropractor in the States gave me the name of one in Paris, so after our game near the French border, we drove to Gérald's apartment. He answered the door at 3 a.m., his eyes puffy with sleep, and smiled. After a quick crack, I felt better for a few days. But the headache and heartache returned.

Vonnie nagged me like a mother hen, making sure I never overdid it. On days we had practice, she made me skip classes. Every morning she ran in the woods and I wrote, feeling wistful that I could no longer run, nor play pick-up games. My energy had to be conserved for enduring practice and the Saturday game. Gradually as the day wore on, the pain in my neck and at the back of my skull became intolerable. I spent an inordinate amount of time lying flat on back to ease the endless ache in my head and shoulder.

If I could make it to Christmas, I was sure Gérald and my chiropractor in Paris could soothe the pain. Even within the security of Gérald's bachelor pad, my head still spun. I tied a blue band over my eyes and forced myself to type without looking down at the keys, for, whenever I did the nerves to my brain became pinched and I couldn't think or see clearly.

My brain was choking. The ink blurred. Answer me, paper, with your blank whiteness, am I going crazy? I felt drunk. No, even worse, I felt high and I couldn't come back down unless I saw a chiro and he put my head back on straight. For a while I felt alert. Alive. Then my head started sliding off my shoulder and I was gone again.

I took the train to Paris for the holidays, but The Grinch stole Christmas. Gérald insisted I pick out my own present. Christmas in Paris, bah humbug. But the weekend in Normandy meeting Gérald's family was magic. In France, the holiday wasn't under the tree, but on the table. The French eat their presents, stuffed goose liver, raw oysters, caviar—all the delicacies I disliked. And New Year's Eve was another eating orgy with Gérald's relatives.

Then I was back on the train for Marburg, scribbling in my notebook. Words were my only contact with reality. After three weeks in France, I found myself thinking in French, dreaming in German. Go on, girl. Pack your bag. Don't look back. You'll never miss love; you are love. You take it with you; you leave it behind. It's all you have to give.

As soon as Vonnie got back from the States, she burst into the apartment and closed all the shutters.

"What are you doing?" I asked, "It's sunny for once."

"I don't want anyone to know we're home," she said. "Put the coffee on."

Then we sipped coffee and ate a box of her mom's homemade cookies while she explained her secrecy. "I don't want anyone ringing that bell till I've hidden my American passport."

"Vonnie, you're getting paranoid."

"I sent my Russian passport by registered mail; I was afraid to carry it with me. But if I left it here, somebody could find it."

"Vonnie, I think we should open the shutters," I said. "People will think you're working for the KGB."

"This is serious. They could put me behind bars!"

On Sundays when I woke up after the game, my body ached so badly, I felt like I'd been sacked a dozen times in a football match. In practice, I stopped in the middle of drills to reach down to touch my toes, hoping to keep the back muscles loose enough to be able to get down on defense. I let free balls roll in front of me, gave up baselines, and sidestepped block-outs on the boards. In scrimmages, I jogged down the court, hating myself for playing so lackadaisically. I kept hearing my grandpa, dad and Phil shouting, "If you aren't going to work out hard, then don't work out at all." For safety, I had to go against every principle I'd ever learned. Midway through practice, I'd take myself out of the scrimmage. "Can you go ten minutes?" my coach asked.

I shook my head and went to the locker-room to hide my tears of pain and shame under a shower of steam. The irony of my situation was excruciating. The little girl, who grew up on the sideline, spent her lifetime searching for this ideal place where the girls were golden and the boys cheered, but then my body, trained to perfection, broke down. I begged God to please let me finish the season. But staying in shape meant doing little in practice so that my spine could hold me up straight at the end of the day. I knew this had to be my last year playing ball and Gérald and I had agreed that I would move to France next season and look for a real job.

In the morning I gazed out of my apartment window at the countryside on the edge of Marburg. Ice, like jewels, adorned the barren trees. A snow-covered slope arched up toward the baby blue horizons where the earth appeared to end at the top of the valley. In the morning I was content until pain shot down my right shoulder, creeping up the back of my head. By late afternoon my mood darkened along with the setting sun, as the throbbing penetrated my muscles.

When I was growing up, I made up stories about my other self — an elegant, feminine woman. Then in France, I became Patricia. I fell in love with china and champagne and men, who were much more manly than any other guys I'd ever known because they weren't afraid to be tender, gentle, even domestic.

In Germany, I became Patty Baby, a tomboy with a French twist. I wore eyeliner with my jeans and high tops and bobbed into the gym and cheered over little boys making baskets. My friends were golden. We laughed and hugged and captured every moment, knowing this time was too priceless to last.

Was I losing my mind? I fought my rising fear with Phil's prophecy. "You are lucky to live and be loved in three worlds." The love, the contact with others, kept me from giving up, from going insane.

"You are an accident waiting to happen," my chiro had warned when he saw me last summer.

He was wrong. I couldn't wait. Life and love beckoned me. Against all my superstitions, I packed my bags for Paris two days before leaving, and then lay awake nights wishing time could hurry up.

"I thought you said it never snowed here," Vonnie complained as we trudged home from practice in a blizzard.

"It didn't last year," I said my stomach gnawing with hunger. I was tempted to bite into the sugarcoated rooftops of the gingerbread houses lining the cobblestone streets.

In the winter of 1983, while we blazed a trail of fire in gyms across Germany, the land remained frozen. Homeless Europeans died in city streets. The snow-covered countryside melted and froze and melted again, spilling out of the waterways that crisscrossed France. Rivers and streams pummeled over embankments toward the sea, devouring everything in their paths. And on the morning of February 10th, the phone in our apartment rang, startling me. Who could be calling so early? I threw off my quilt, cursing.

"Allo," I answered, half asleep, standing barefooted on the icy linoleum floor in the drafty hallway.

"*C'est moi.*"

"Why are you calling now? I'll be there later today."

"Don't drive here," Gérald pleaded. "It's snowing hard!"

"Don't be silly. We waited a year for the team to get us a car. It's automatic for the dumb Americans. Besides I won't be alone. Vonnie will do most of the driving."

"Can't you take the train?"

"I've got all my junk packed. Everything I own is going in that car. It'll be that much easier at the end of the season when I move to Paris. I won't have the team car then."

"Please, take the train."

"We're picking up our car in an hour—be on the road by 9:00 a.m. I'll be in your arms when you get home from work."

"Pat, please be careful. *Je t'aime*"

"*Moi aussi. A bientôt.*"

That ill-fated day, we ignored the storm warnings when we loaded the car for our weekend visit in Paris.

I hung up the phone, walked into the kitchen nook, lit the gas stove, and put on the red kettle for coffee. I sat on the countertop in front of the kitchen window and watched snowflakes drift to the ground while I waited for Vonnie to wake up. Then, we took the bus into town to pick up the car our basketball manager had finally agreed to provide for us.

"About time! We asked for a car in September and it's already February," Vonnie, grumbled while we waited for our new used car to pass inspection. "The Germans love their rules."

"Yeah, but I guess it's for the best," I said, as we stood outside the driver's bureau check point while our lime green VW Passat went through the safety inspections.

When the authorities finally gave us our car keys, we took off winding through the snow-covered hills of Hessen toward Frankfurt. When we got to Giessen, only 25 kilometers away, I got out the map because we were already lost.

"Autobahn is marked with blue signs," I said.

"We should have stayed in Frankfurt after the game last night. We would have been that much closer to Paris."

"We could have celebrated," I said thinking of our victory and remembering the way the ball floated from my fingertips into the baskets just like the old days before I injured my spine.

"How's your back?" Vonnie asked, reading my mind.

"Like always after a game. Feels like I got hit by a truck."

"I told you to stay away from the boards. Tomorrow you can go to your chiropractor," said Vonnie. "Who would have ever thought it would be so hard to find a chiropractor in Europe?"

I crawled into the back seat next to my guitar and settled into my special chiropractic pillow. At the French border I popped up for passport control.

After we passed the tollbooth at Metz, Vonnie burst out laughing, and from the back seat I saw her shoulder length black hair bob up and down as her body shook with laughter. "Jeez, the French love rules too. You see that cop pointing at my seatbelt?"

"He was waving you over to the side of the road. They fine you for driving without seat belts."

"I've got it on now, so he can point at somebody else."

"You tired? You want me to drive?"

"No, I'm fine."

Later, Vonnie's voice interrupted my nap, "You want this Bavarian cream sandwich?"

"Huh? No," I mumbled and dozed off, dreaming of last night's victory. I leaped to catch the pass and jump-stopped to a halt, ending the fast break in mid-flight. While my head and shoulders leaned right, my feet and hips drove left. I glided past my opponent with one quick dribble, shoved off my inside foot and lunged toward the basket with all my force; yet I released the ball so gently it kissed the backboard and swished through the net without touching the rim.

One minute I was on top of the world with the all-powerful high of the victorious athlete, and the next instant my omnipotence dissolved as I flew weightlessly through the sky. Vonnie screamed. I folded into the fetal position, wrapping my pillow over my head. Then I slammed into hard metal. When I regained consciousness, icy water sucked my breath away.

"Swim, Pat, swim!" Vonnie shouted from the embankment. Sound muffled as if my head was stuffed with feathers. I pulled my arms forward; a knife of pain stabbed my chest.

"Swim! Get out!"

I coughed and spit blood. Cold water numbed my limbs. My mind shut down. A force pulled me toward a deep, dark hole, but Vonnie's voice beckoned me back.

"Pat, swim! Move!" Vonnie's screams flashed like a warning signal.

Vonnie crouched on land with one arm extended, repeating my name like a prayer. I focused on my best friend's voice and reached out instinctively toward the comforting sound.

My arms flailed at the water and slapped at Vonnie's outstretched hand. Vonnie clasped my wrist. As the current propelled me forward, Vonnie dug her heels into the soft snow and leaned back until she was sitting. Using her powerful shoulders and back muscles, Vonnie pulled me onto the snowy shore and helped me stumble up the steep embankment to the side of the *Autobahn*. While Vonnie waved her arms frantically at the motorists speeding past, I crouched in the snow at her feet in a wet bundle of wool. Vonnie scrambled down the embankment toward the river.

"Vonnie, don't leave me," I shouted into the wind. Vonnie stopped and turned, cupping her hands around her mouth.

"I have to get into the car, to get Gérald's number. We have to call," Vonnie pleaded.

"Vonnie, stop! You can't swim. I know Gérald's number."

"Mon dieu! Qu'est ce qui se passe?" I looked up toward the man's voice. Someone finally stopped.

"Help! She can't walk," Vonnie demanded, running towards me. Vonnie folded me into her arms and carried me to the side of his car. "Get her to a hospital! "

"Vous ne pouvez pas rentrer dans ma voiture," he said. *"Ce n'est pas la mienne. Elle est à la societé."*

"Oh, my God," I thought. "We're going to die here on the side of a barren highway in a foreign land."

"He can't, it's a company car," I translated for Vonnie.

"What the hell do you mean it's a company car?" Vonnie yelled with her fists balled in rage.

"Vonnie, this is France. He can't understand English. Shut up and pray."

No sooner had Vonnie fallen to her knees than a police car stopped. The heavyset officer took his lined police jacket off and pulled it over my shoulders. While Vonnie yelled at them in English, I begged in broken French, *"Hospital. Vite."*

"We aren't allowed to transport accident victims. An ambulance is on the way," he apologized in French.

When the ambulance arrived, the men lifted me onto the stretcher, and I took one last look at the surreal picture of the smashed Volkswagen, half-submerged in floodwaters. Two men in white uniforms took off our heavy, wet sweaters and jeans and covered us in scratchy old military blankets.

"Oh, là, là, elle est grande," said one man. *"Quelle belle plante."*

"Oh là, là, les français, " I thought. "It can't be that bad, if they're calling me a tall, pretty plant." But still, I could not stop trembling and Vonnie would not stop ranting.

"Calmez-vous," they insisted. But I shook so hard I feared I'd die in the back of the beat-up old ambulance that felt like a refrigerated ice cream truck.

In the hospital they laid me on an icy metallic table. I was swimming again, this time in a sea of whiteness. White walls. White sheets. White faces. White hands. I shook so badly, the doctors had to wait until I recovered from shock before taking X-rays. They wheeled me into a room and wrapped me in blankets and a heating pad.

"I looked back and saw your guitar, but you were gone.

You must have flown out the window when we flipped," Vonnie said. "There were no doors back there. You would have been trapped in the car. We're lucky to be alive."

I didn't feel lucky, I felt like dying. My body was a giant bruise, a purple mass of pain, my head a lump of mush. Every time I inhaled, it felt like a fat man was jumping on my chest. My stomach contracted in spasms.

"I never even got wet," Vonnie babbled from the bed next to me. "I was ejected before we hit water. It's a miracle we survived!"

"You should've waited till the weather warmed up for swimming," a petite, dark-eyed nurse kidded when she brought Vonnie's dinner.

I begged for something to kill the pain.

"Doctor say no medicine. Hospital wine no good," the nurse said. She returned with a plastic baby sipper cup filled from a private stock. "*A votre santé,*" she said, cradling me in one arm and tilting the cup to my lips with the other. I sipped the ruby liquid and tried to suppress the fear that my life would never be normal again.

"Where's the jelly?" Vonnie griped.

"No one in France eats jelly on bread at dinner."

"If I'm stuck here, I should get to eat what I want. Ask the nurse for jelly."

"Shut up," I wanted to say, but bit my tongue, grateful for the distraction from the pain. When the nurse returned I had my own requests. "I have to call my boyfriend."

"You can't walk and there's no phone in the room."

"He's waiting. We should have been in Paris hours ago."

The nurse disappeared and returned wheeling a cart. With Vonnie's help, the nurse eased me off the bed onto the gurney and then rolled me to the nurses' station to use the phone. I couldn't lift myself up, so the nurse dialed the phone for me.

"Gérald," I blurted, bursting in tears at the sound of his voice.

"Pat, what happened? Where are you?"

"In the hospital. *Viens. Vite.* Get me out!"

"*Oh mon dieu!* Are you okay? Is Vonnie okay?"

"No," I cried. The nurse removed the phone from my hand and explained that we were in the hospital in Verdun and then hung up. "I have to say goodbye." I moaned as they wheeled me back to my room.

"Shush," the nurse said, brushing a wisp of brown hair from my blue eyes. "*Demain.* He come. *Calmez-vous.*"

"Don't sleep," Vonnie said. "You might go into a coma."

Vonnie, like a sentry guarding the fortress, kept vigil. Every minute she interrupted the silence. "Pat, stay awake!"

No way could I sleep. I moaned through the night, gripping my stomach. The next day, doctors stuck a tube in my nose to pump out my stomach and another in my arm to feed me. They explained that my bowels had stopped functioning from the blow to my back, but I only understood that I was confined to a hospital bed while machines took over the functions my body could no longer perform.

Vonnie, suffering from minor bruises, was being released. Our German team manager came to pick her up and straighten out the paperwork. Neither of us had health insurance. The jovial police officer wandered in and out of the room carrying my waterlogged guitar, books, clothes, papers, and pieces of my life that they found floating down La Meuse River.

"How's the Mermaid?" he teased. "*Ça va?*"

"*Ça va, ça va,*" I lied. "Did you find my passport?"

"Not yet, frogmen are in the water now looking," he said. "Can I ask a few questions for the police report?"

While I translated in broken French, Vonnie explained that she thought she was driving about 80 mph when she fell asleep at the wheel. After the police left, the nurse hung my clothes and notebooks in front of the electric heaters to dry.

Vonnie held up my heavy wool sweater. She peeked through the bullet holes drilled by the churning river current over rocks and asked, "Sure you want to keep this?"

I shook my head. "Aren't you going home today?"

"I'm not leaving. They can't throw me out!" Vonnie signed the hospital release papers, but when it was time to leave, she refused to budge. "I'm staying to take care of you." Her black eyes locked with my blue ones in a stubborn showdown of wills.

"Vonnie, the season isn't over. The team needs you more than I do. We don't have insurance. Who will pay the hospital bill, especially with all you eat?" I asked. How could I explain I didn't want to see my best friend, to be reminded that she could walk and I could not? All season Vonnie worried about my safety and my bad back, directing me out of traffic on the court. In my mind, I knew the crash was an accident, but in my heart I blamed her. I needed time to forgive.

The nurse left, then our manager left, and reluctantly, Vonnie followed them out the door. Water dripped from a faucet and haunting moans echoed down the deserted corridor.

At regular intervals, as if in training, I swung my arms in circles at my sides, while my spine remained pinned to the white sheets. I cocked my wrist and shot imaginary jumpers into the air, snapping my wrist, checking the follow through. Swish. I still had the touch. But what had happened to my legs? My long, muscular legs lay idle, slowly succumbing to atrophy. My best feature failed me. I closed my eyes as my legs danced across the polished hardwood floor toward the hoop.

In reality, I was again pinned in my crib with my feet locked in iron traction bars at one end of the bed and my head trapped in metal at the other; I was going nowhere. My throat and nose were raw from the feeding tubes that sustained my life. My head throbbed; my back ached. I longed to escape the confines of a body that no longer worked.

The impact of my curled body hitting hard metal literally broke me in half. My sternum cracked. I had compressed fractures of my dorsal vertebrae. Bruises the size of grapefruits covered my shoulders, elbows and knees, but my fighting spirit remained intact.

"I'll show them," I thought, gritting my teeth. "I'll make a comeback. I worked too hard; I'm not giving up now." Through broken bones, torn ligaments, and shattered spirit, I always picked myself up after a fall.

No normal human beings should have survived the impact or the relentless current when our car flipped off the French autoroute, sailed over a 100-meter high embankment and crashed into La Meuse River. But then, we were not normal. As pro ball players, the muscles of our 25-year-old bodies had been honed to perfection, trained to withstand trauma.

In seconds, years of training meant nothing; I was reduced to an invalid. If I pulled up on the triangular bar hanging overhead and wriggled my upper body, I could peek over the window ledge at the red rooftops of Verdun. Graveyards covered the hillside of the famous WWI look-out point. Why wasn't I buried beside yesterday's heroes? I had lost my possessions, my job, my identity, and my purpose. What was left? Life.

Chapter 13: Transition

Paris, fall 1983

"My doctors told me I would never walk again. My mother told me I would. I believed my mother. The triumph can't be had without the struggle. And I know what struggle is. I have spent a lifetime trying to share what it has meant to be a woman first in the world of sports so that other young women have a chance to reach their dreams."
Wilma Rudolph
The "fastest woman in the world" at the 1960 Olympics and winner of three gold medals wore metal braces on her legs as a child.

I was sure that once I escaped the hospital, everything would return to normal. But the euphoria at being released was short-lived as I struggled to fit into a French bachelor's pad, Gérald's studio apartment.

"What is this?" Gérald asked, stabbing the steak. "A hockey puck?"

"Don't like it, cook it yourself," I snapped. "Americans don't eat raw meat." I shoved my plate away, hobbled to the side of the room and flopped onto the bed, aggravated there was nowhere to run. Gérald left the table and sat down next to me.

"No one wants me here," I said. "I have to leave the country every three months to get my passport stamped or they'll throw me out of France. The team can't hire me without a work permit. And I can't get a work permit without residency papers."

"We're getting married. Then you'll be legal."

"I don't want to have to get married for the damn bureaucracy." I stood up and paced, trying to stop the room from spinning. "I speak French like a baby. The only job I can get is coaching. I don't want to coach; I want to play."

"You'll only be coaching six hours a week," Gérald said, trying to soothe me. "People work eight hours a day at a job they can't stand!"

"I promised you'd never see me cry again," I sniffled as I

slammed the bathroom door, wiping my tears on the sleeve of my old gray sweatshirt. I would never confess to the number of nights I crept from the bedroom to the bathroom and lay on the cold tile sobbing and sinking deeper into isolation.

"We can work this out," Gérald coaxed.

"It is *your* job, *your* family, *your* country," I said later, tracing his cheek with my finger. "Now I am just a spectator. No one can help me run again; no one can stop the pain."

"Please, don't give up. We'll try another doctor."

After every breakdown, the emotional release left me tranquilized. Before I fell asleep that night I prayed for a purpose, for peace of mind. I drifted to sleep and dreamed of writing my story, a testimony of faith in the face of adversity, as a pioneer in women's sports.

Every time I sat down to type, the typewriter keys blurred. I twisted my body into different positions to keep the pressure off my spine. I typed lying down flat on the couch with my head hanging over the end to prevent nerves in my neck from being pinched. Headaches, like red ants, marched from the back of my head to my eyes. I pounded the typewriter keys, trying to release my frustration onto the page, but my heart didn't pump faster, I didn't sweat, and I didn't get a physical rush like I did running on the basketball court.

I saw another specialist who prescribed tranquilizers and pain pills. I threw them away. Pain defined my limits and kept me from self-destructing. No drug could replace the joy of movement.

Every day I typed for fifteen minutes until the pressure started building in my head. Then I put on a Michael Jackson tape, strapped one-pound weights to my ankles, picked up two-pound dumbbells and tried to exercise away my frustration. By inhaling more air, I hoped some of it would reach my brain. But when I stopped, the room continued moving. Books on the desk swayed. When I looked at the poster on the wall, the model's hair wavered. Though the music had stopped, the tape still seemed to spin around.

"Aha, I see," the neurologist said, his fuzzy eyebrows like caterpillars arched above his black glasses. His eyes twitched as he observed me hop on one leg in my underwear. Then, he hooked me to an electroencephalograph that would monitor the electrodes to my brain, and he attached wires to parts of my hand, back and head. Gérald squeezed my hand as the shocks seared through my right side when the doctor administered jolts of electricity. The specialist read the results and blinked.

"There is damage to the right side," he announced. "But a nerve grows one hundredth of a millimeter weekly. You should regain sensation in your right hand and arm. The pathology is not permanent. A psychiatrist could help."

"I don't need a shrink. He does," I shouted at Gérald as I stomped out the door. "Not serious! Why the hell does the room move, my ears pop, my scalp tingle?"

Residents returning from work, stared at the ranting woman slumped in the corridor of their apartment building.

"Pat, *calmes-toi*," Gérald nudged me into the elevator where I wanted to remain forever, bouncing off the padded walls.

When we finally reached the apartment at 10 p.m., I stood beside the empty refrigerator.

"I tried to buy meat," I blurted, shaking in fear of disappointing the man I loved, "the butcher's wasn't open until late afternoon." It drove me crazy how all the shops closed for lunch in the middle of the day. I bit my tongue to keep from screaming, "I hate my role as wifey." If I alienated Gérald, I would sever the sole link to my sanity.

"I'll make an omelet,'" Gérald said, embracing me.

We ate the warm eggs in silence, and then curled up together in a cocoon of stormy love. My rage, his calm. Complete. Almost.

In the morning, I typed. In the afternoon, I swam laps or walked the mile to my physical therapist in Paris. I had no insurance to reimburse medical costs. My therapist, the trainer for a men's basketball team, treated me for free. After he showed me which back strengthening exercises to do, I worked out on my own. In front of mirror-covered walls, I lifted 3-pound weights as if preparing for an Olympic trial.

Even on my worst days, I realized that by surviving the accident, God gave me a second chance. My existence was too precious to threaten by purging. Also, in France food is sacred and living with a Frenchman, I knew that I would never miss a meal again.

I awoke to the chirping of birds and hoped the change in seasons would bring a change in health. I attacked the day, trying to get everything done before the crushing pain in the middle of my back and the spinning room made me so dizzy that I had to lie down again. I resumed my position lying flat on my back, looking up, and praying. "Please make it stop hurting. " By evening, I wanted to fall asleep quickly, to begin a new day, so I could enjoy a few pain-free early morning hours before the crippling aches forced me back to bed.

Each morning I vowed to attack the day, hoping this would be the day I won. I fought bravely, but often ended up hurting myself by lifting too many weights, typing too many paragraphs, or walking too far, always trying to prove to myself that I could live a normal life. Then my head slid off the left side of my shoulder. My jaw locked. My ears popped and my eyes darted back and forth until the whole world was moving like a woman swinging her hips in high heels. My mind deceived me by moving objects, distorting sounds, and altering my emotions until I was out of control. Every day I walked to exhaustion, trying to escape the walls of the apartment that seemed to be closing in on me.

On a sunny day, Paris in the springtime was a song, a melody of movement. Window shutters popped open and clothes hung out to dance in the breeze. In the parks, gardens exploded into fireworks of spring in pink, yellow, and red blossoms.

Children in knickers chased soccer balls while old men in berets and button-down sweater vests played *boules*. Businessmen strode by, coattails and ties flying, overcoats abandoned. Legs bared above the knee strolled past, luring second glances from passersby who stopped to admire the latest Parisian fashion. Men smiled — the mini-skirt was back.

Round-bellied retirees huffed and puffed at the heels of their German shepherds and frail, high-heeled, old ladies tottered behind their poodles. On every street corner corduroy-clothed baby carriages collided and housewives peeked under hand-knitted blankets to admire the cuddly bundles ol' man winter delivered to the neighbors. At the Metro entrance, bag ladies hung their tattered sweaters on the station signposts. In abandoned lots, winos dragged rusty pots from makeshift huts to air in the sunlight. Even the bums were spring-cleaning.

In the fruit and vegetable stands, lettuce leaves popped open and tomatoes ripened in their crates while oranges and grapefruit rolled to the back row to make room for the strawberries. Under the direction of the spring sun, the city became a symphony of color and movement. Paris in springtime was like remembering the long forgotten line to a childhood lyric. Suddenly every heart was humming its own favorite tune.

At odds with my body, I was the only one in Paris who was off-beat. Phone calls from Germany and the United States interrupted my solitude. I assured loved ones that I was doing fine, but as soon as I hung up the phone, I wondered. I watched myself and shook my head thinking "oh well, she'll work it out." Then I realized the "she" was "me" and I panicked. Would I ever piece back together my broken life?

As always, letters and calls left me feeling lonely and homesick, but the home I missed the most was the hardwood. In a suitcase career where I left places without time to say good-bye, basketball was my only constant. In my daily bout with self-pity, I felt my muscles succumbing to fat, my mind invaded by worry. I longed for the comfort of my first love. Nothing filled my heart as completely as an empty hoop in a deserted gym where I could shoot baskets until I felt peaceful.

Gérald, understanding what my words could not explain, took me in his arms, cradled me gently and whispered, "I am the constant in your life now."

Though I found comfort in his arms, as a dying athlete, what I really longed for was movement.

During the day I fought to regain use of my muscles. I was no longer training to drive the baseline or sprint down the court, but conditioning for survival—to sit up straight and to walk to the store. I struggled to accept my limitations, knowing that I would never be able to compete in sports again. But at night I dreamed I was running down court, leaping for the pass and gliding toward the hoop, my arms thrown up toward the heavens, my perfect shot, an offering to the heavens. Then I would wake up in a cold sweat, my arms heavy, my palms filled with fingernail indentations from my clenched fists, my heart aching as though someone dear had just died. I would cry, mourning my loss of self, myself, the athlete.

Years of conditioning kept me disciplined, so I stretched and exercised religiously, but I felt hopeless. Before, I had always trained for the next season. Now, I continued to go through the motions without any motivation because my life lacked a goal. One day, when lamenting what I could not do and wondering what to do with my life, my physical therapist said, "Call Henry, he'll help you out."

"Who's Henry?"

"You don't know Henry? He's the father of French basketball, the first American to come over here. He's the go-between for all the teams and players," he said. "Here's his number at the American School of Paris where he teaches."

The next day, my hand shook as I dialed the number.

"McKinzie? Yeah, I remember you. Played for Asnières a couple years ago. Shot the eyes out of the basket. Need a job?" Henry said with a laugh. "Great! We need a basketball coach."

Me? Coach? I never wanted to coach; I only wanted to play. I did not want to follow in my dad and grandfather's footsteps, such giant footsteps to fill. The football field at Eureka College and baseball field at NIU bore the McKinzie name. How could I teach other people about basketball? I only knew how to play.

Call it serendipity. Call it divine intervention. But every time my life hit a roadblock, someone pointed out the detour and got me back on track. In 1983, Henry Fields, was that someone.

When I walked into the gym at the American School of Paris, an international school, and saw those girls in every shape and color with African and Asian and Scandinavian and Germanic features, I knew I could turn them into a team. I could combine their differences to complement one another. I could inspire these girls to believe, to fight adversity, to grow up and go on.

So I blew the whistle and called them together. "I'm Pat, your new coach," I began to say in a shaky voice. "My grandfather was a coach, my dad was a coach, and my best friend is a coach. I used to play professional basketball—in the States, in France, in Germany. A car accident ended my career. I can't play anymore, but I know the game. That is my gift to you. In return, you will play with all your heart whenever you walk onto the court. Let's go."

At the end of my first practice as a coach, after the last player had left the locker room, I sat down at the free throw line. A sunbeam reflected through the window creating a shadow over the hoop. It looked like a halo. Home sweet hardwood. Thank God, I *was* still in the game.

A whistle shrieked. Feet stopped shuffling. The man on the end of the bench quickly unfolded his long legs, stood, and shouted, "*Ce n'est pas vrai.* Ref, ya gotta be kidding."

The short, little, bald, French referee glared up at the big,

Black basketball coach and said, "Henry, *calmes-toi*. Sit down."

But as soon as the next bad call was made, Henry was on his feet again, throwing his arms up and yelling, "Ref. Be serious. He didn't touch the guy." As soon as the game was over, win or lose, Henry's gold front tooth sparkled and his brown eyes twinkled as he would say, "C'mon ref, I'll buy ya a drink." Henry was friends with everybody, even the bad refs.

The 6'5", 190-pound former star center — with hands big enough to palm a ball, feet wide enough to cut off a baseline, and a heart warm enough to win over a country — became the Father of French Basketball. With his long, gangly arms, Henry embraced me into the fold of expat former pros by showing me the ropes of coaching in international ball. Yet, our friendship would never have developed without my family's upbringing that taught me tolerance and appreciation of all people, regardless of race.

Life may not be fair, but great coaches are. Grandpa Mac taught fairness by his actions more than his words. When my dad, an All-American at NIU, argued during a game while playing for Grandpa, he was benched. It did not matter who he was. My dad instilled those same values of treating others equally in me. So did the President, who never passed up an opportunity to publically thank his old coach for his role in the lives of young men.

"I played football with Franklin Burkhardt, a center. Burgie and I remained lifelong friends. It wasn't so easy for a young Black man to come to college and make his way back in that day," President Reagan recounted at the Timmie Awards, "Dr. Burkhardt went on to become the athletic director at Moorhead State. Before he died, Burgie said something most fitting for the man I am about to introduce, the man who had the most influence in my entire life — Coach Ralph McKinzie.'"

That was the kind of coach I wanted to be, too. So if I was going to be a coach, I was more than willing to learn from a Black coach who was dubbed the Father of French Basketball.

Chapter 14: My Greatest Loss

Wisconsin, summer 1983

"It is worth remembering that the time of greatest gain in terms of wisdom and inner strength is often that of greatest difficulty."

Dalai Lama

In July, Gérald flew to Chicago to meet my family. We spent a week at the cottage on Summit Lake. I was filled with happiness sharing my sacred spot with the man I cherished at the place where I felt so empowered by the spirit of my ancestors, especially my grandparents. Even though it wasn't planned, we were thrilled when I found out that I was pregnant. Just as the woods guarded our little red cabin, so joy sheltered our heart. While I picked berries, Gérald chopped wood. At night, we curled in front of the crackling fire where we warmed our bodies by the hearth, our hearts by our dreams. After the last embers died out, Gérald lay awake rubbing my tummy, making sure "junior" was still there. In the morning as the sun peeked through the curtains, Gérald kissed my belly.

We wore matching silly grins, as though we were children sharing a secret. I gazed across the shimmering lake that reflected my childhood memories: sandcastles, tree forts, tubing, floating, and boating. Now I dreamed of how the child growing in me would one day love those same things.

I was so content, I ignored the pain that night—until I started bleeding. When it didn't stop, I called a doctor.

"You might be losing the baby," he said in a semi-sleep stupor. "Nothing to do, but to let nature take its course. If the bleeding gets worse, lie down, and put your feet up."

The next morning, the brilliant sun beaming across the silver lake illuminated our fears. By noon, every minute a contraction wracked my body. With each stabbing pain, I screamed. Gérald stifled my anguished cries, "Breathe slowly."

"Go out for fresh air," I begged. Instead he opened the window shade in the somber room. A beam of sunlight spewed through the trees, spraying hope across the room. I prayed into the ray of light, "Please let my baby live." But as my body became one with the pain, so my mind became one with the reality, my baby was dying.

"Breathe, calm," Gérald pleaded. With each new stabbing contraction, I lost a little more lifeblood. I sat on the toilet seat and shrieked as the clots of blood poured from my loins into my hands. Gérald tenderly removed the deformed fetus from my fingers and placed it in a jar as the doctor had instructed.

My blood pressure dropped. My breathing became shallow. Terrified, Gérald wrapped me in a sheet and laid me in the back of the car. While he maneuvered the Malibu around the winding back road, toward the nearest hospital an hour away, I muffled screams of pain by concentrating on the green treetops as they blurred into the purple sky.

At the hospital, nurses laid me on an icy table in a room as cold as a morgue. A steady stream of nurses entered and exited, assuring me that nothing could be done to stop the pain. They interrupted my cries with questions. I wanted to scream in their faces. "Leave me alone. My baby is dying."

I shivered. I thought I was going into shock from the cold and exhaustion. "You're doing fine," one nurse said.

Years of competition taught me to endure pain. Never in any sport had I experienced a pain as intense as the one defeating me now. I anticipated our baby's birth as a moment more triumphant than any championship. The delivery would be like running a marathon—I would control my pace, breathing, and concentration. But the pain was more excruciating than that last quarter of a mile kick and now there would be no reward at the finish.

Gérald squeezed my hand. I clung to him as though clinging to life. I breathed deeply as the spasms overtook my body. Then suddenly, the pain stopped. I felt peaceful and light, as though I were floating.

"It's not your fault. Usually a miscarriage occurs because the embryo is deformed," the doctor explained. "A spontaneous abortion is nature's blessing in disguise."

I blamed myself. I alone dropped the ball, missed the last shot, lost our first child. Silent tears rolled down my cheeks and, for the first time, I ached for Gérald, not myself. He witnessed my pain knowing the end result of my suffering would be our sorrow.

"Would you like to keep the fetus?" the doctor asked gently.

Gérald, horrified, shook his head.

Back at the cabin, I called family and friends. Nobody knew what to say. The silence magnified my guilt. Just as I wanted to shout to the world that I was pregnant, I wanted to announce my miscarriage. I hoped that by speaking openly, I might meet someone who had experienced the same loss, shared the same guilt. My anguish forced me to want to talk about what most women hide in humiliation.

Though the doctor assured me that 20 percent of all pregnancies ended in miscarriages, regardless of what the woman does, I blamed myself. I followed the guidelines for a healthy pregnancy more strictly than training rules in sports. No alcohol. No smoking. No drugs. Lots of rest and proteins and exercise. Despite all my deliberation, my baby died. No matter how hard my family tried to convince me otherwise, I felt like I had fumbled the football at the goal line of the Super Bowl. I, alone, was responsible for carrying our baby.

"I've lost everything," I whimpered in Gérald's arms.

"Not everything," Gérald whispered, "you still have me."

The following days were blurred with a new pain, a hollow emptiness like the flu that settled into each muscle fiber, making my whole body ache. I woke at night and felt for my belly that was no longer there. I clutched my breasts trying to hang on to their fullness, and I asked Gérald, "Why?"

Instead of answers, he offered strong arms to embrace my anger at the unanswerable, when I burst into tears at the sight of a pregnant woman, and the laughter of children made me melancholy.

Despite his compassion, I paced around the cabin in a quiet rage. Suddenly I abhorred this place of childhood joy. "Why has God tainted this spot with death?" I thought. "How could I feel so full of life one day and so empty the next?"

No doctor on earth could give me the answer. If there was an answer, I could only find it here at the lake. Here, where the eerie stillness of the night pierced by the loon's cry, breaks into pink and gold dawn filled with the chatter of chipmunks. This, too, must be part of the plan.

Every evening when the great orange sun sank behind the green tree line, when the wind nestled into the blue spruce for the night, transforming the lake into glass, I rowed into the cove and spoke to my grandma whose spirit remained deep within the woods.

"How could you survive the loss of two sons," I wondered, "one stillborn baby and another at eighteen months—killed when a stranger's fireworks tossed into a crowd at a parade exploded at his feet?"

"Help me," I sobbed. Grandma echoed, "Help me."

I was not alone.

Grandma lived a happy, full life. Her faith helped her endure the sorrow. Grandma survived; I would too. She prevented bitterness by investing in others. It wasn't until I suffered the greatest of all losses, that I truly understood my grandparents' sacrifices.

I sat in the cabin staring at the memorabilia hanging on the knotted-pine walls. I gazed from the old black and white photographs of Camp Ney-A-Ti to the framed colored prints of my grandparents and Reagan at Grandpa's retirement dinner, in the Oval Office and at the Timmie Awards. I wondered how my grandparents could remain so dedicated to teaching in the face of their losses?

"As athletes, we knew Coach could outrun and out-hit us at practice but it wasn't until later, as men with children of our own, that we really understood his strength," Reagan recounted in his speech at my grandpa's NIU and Eureka College's testimonial dinner. "Before my senior year of college, Mac's son was killed accidently during Eureka's 4th of July celebration. That fall when football started again, Coach Mac resumed his job making men out of other people's sons."

When Reagan lost the first election, he ran again crediting my grandfather with giving him the courage to keep fighting in the face of adversity. I knew what he meant. When my professional basketball career ended, my grandpa encouraged me to stay in the game. But now I had lost the will to go on.

Though I knew I had inherited my grandparents' resiliency, I felt so empty that I prayed to the Great Spirit for strength to go on. When it was time to leave, I felt like I was leaving a part of myself behind. When we had arrived, we were three. Now we were only two. Nobody would notice the difference. No one would mourn a death that most had not yet considered life. We came to the cabin as excited children anxious to play house; we left as weary adults, disillusioned with the game. A baby should have been born with bright eyes reflecting his parents' love. Instead, Daddy's eyes were browner; Mommy's eyes were bluer. How could I endure the greatest of losses?

Chapter 15: Whole New Ball Game

Paris, autumn 1984

We are together,
My child and I,
Mother and child, yes,
But sisters really
Against whatever denies
Us all that we are.

-Alice Walker

When we returned to Paris in late August, I was still mourning. In part, I pined for my old self, the athlete. My inability to run or to play basketball—or any ball game for that matter—left me feeling sad and bitter. During my athletic career, I endured championship title upsets in overtime, last second shots falling short at the buzzer, winning seasons ending in defeat, yet no loss could compare to the emptiness that permeated every cell when I lost my baby. The pain of loss was accentuated by a sense of failure to fulfill my destiny as a woman. To a girl growing up caught in the crossfire of gender wars of the women's revolution, my inability to carry a fetus to full-term signified the ultimate failure—as if there were inherent flaws in my physical make up. On top of the all-encompassing despair, I endured a self-loathing initiated by a society that had yet to understand the female athlete.

Every month I imagined my belly and breasts swelled, and I was filled with renewed hope until my period started and my dream was deflated. While Gérald worked ten hours a day in the printing business, I settled into a routine. In the mornings, I typed up long journal entries and articles, and the afternoons I spent in the gym, coaching at the American School of Paris. At night I coached a French women's team. But I was still in physical pain from the car accident and brokenhearted from the loss of my baby.

At night as I lay awake waiting for Gerald to return from volleyball practice, I wondered what planetary paths crossed, what cosmic powers collided to unite a small-town Midwestern girl and a Frenchman from the Normandy beaches? In the beginning of our relationship, every time I returned to Paris, it was to say good-bye. I assumed one day I would forget, as I had forgotten all those endearing qualities of other lovers. Even when apart, images of Gérald's dark eyes, his thick curly hair left in a little boy rumple, and his strong shoulders that tapered to his slender waist haunted me. Instead of forgetting, I fell deeper in love.

I waited for him to criticize, complain, demand, or control. Instead, he listened to my problems, supported my interests, and respected my independence. He even helped with the housework. A dream man. A Mr. Right.

Then what was wrong? Why did I pace the apartment, night after night, terrified of my wedding day? Marriage is never an easy decision, especially when signing the contract means living abroad. Indecision ripped my heart to shreds. Gérald, ever supportive, helped me to ease through the transitions from America to France, player to coach. I thanked my lucky stars for bringing him into my life.

A streetlight shimmered through our bedroom window in Paris, filling the cracks in the wooden shutters with dirty yellow bars, accentuating my feeling of imprisonment by my indecision. I thought getting married, like losing one's virginity, was just something that happened—an inevitable occurrence in a woman's life. Yet with my own wedding only weeks away, the doubts haunted me.

I slipped out of the warm bed and padded down the cold tile hallway, pacing four steps from the kitchen to the den. In the beginning, right after my car accident, Gérald's studio apartment had been a haven, this relationship a retreat. Now the room was a cage; my fiancé's love, a shackle.

I was the wrong character in the right story. I grew up in tennis shoes on playing fields of the Midwest. A tomboy. A fighter. Not a lover. Now wearing eyeliner and high heels, I starred in a romance novel in Paris, the City of Lights, in France, the land of love. I never believed in fairytales, but now I intended to marry a man I fell in love with at first sight.

Both of us were skeptical about matrimony. The ceremony—the dress, flowers, dinner, gifts—all seemed superficial. Married by time and circumstance and tragedy, Gérald held my hand when I was machine-fed after my car accident. He cradled my heart when I was hopeless after I lost my firstborn prematurely. We promised to look after one another and sealed our vows with tears. No celebration. Only silent reality. We lived in a cramped apartment, but created space for one another. In order to help pay the bills, I coached. It broke my heart to sit on the bench, so Gérald sat beside me, taking statistics, to help me let go of my dreams of playing. I listened to his frustrations in the business world.

Together we stumbled through the motions of the wedding game. The guests were invited, the dinner was planned, and the ceremony was organized. We knew marriage was a compromise, not a Hawaiian honeymoon. I understood that I forfeited a part of my dream to share his, in hopes that together we could reach once unattainable goals as one.

We wanted a simple ceremony, a cold buffet in Paris with friends, but ended up with a traditional seven-course dinner for the family in Normandy. I longed for my own wedding, but agreed to a double wedding with Gérald's older sister, to help cut down on expenses. I coped with my disappointment by remaining detached.

My strong willed, mother-in-law-to-be had a take-charge personality that belied her petite stature. Every other day Françoise called, asking, "Do you have the documents?"

"What papers?" I feigned ignorance.

"The papers from the American Embassy saying you've never been married before."

Without the perseverance of my mother-in-law, we would still be waiting to complete the official paperwork to this day. I stood in a long line at the Embassy, and then I stepped in front of a lawyer and vowed, "I swear I've never been married before." He stamped the official document. Lo and behold, by simply raising my right hand in oath, I could marry different partners in a half a dozen other countries.

That weekend in Normandy, Françoise served a traditional dinner with plenty of courses, providing ample time to discuss wedding plans. "Have you written your gift list?" She asked.

"All we need is a washing machine," I offered.

"That's not personal. How about picking out china?"

"We don't need china, *Maman*," Gérald said. "Why tell us to make a gift list, if nobody wants to buy what we request?"

"I'd really like a salad spinner," I said. Françoise rolled her eyes. She thought I was being facetious, but I was sincerely fascinated by the way the French prepared lettuce. They soaked the leaves in vinegar water, and then they wrung them out gently like laundry on a delicate spin cycle. Finally each individual leaf was placed on a paper towel and patted dry. No wonder I remained a dismal failure in the kitchen. Their culinary expertise included the savoir-faire of salad spinning.

"Why don't we go look for a wedding dress?" Françoise asked, wringing her hands, fearing her daughter-in-law to-be might show up in a sweat suit.

How could I explain that I was not the traditional wedding type girl? I became the first girl in our town to wear T-shirts to school and pants to church.

"I have my wedding dress," I blurted. "It's blue."

For years, I'd listened to girls talk about their wedding as though it were a quick trip to heaven. My wedding was only two weeks away and both feet remained firmly planted on the ground.

"Let's plan the menu. What would you like to serve?"

"Hamburgers and French fries," I retorted and stomped out into the street with tears streaming down my cheeks. Dirty, gray buildings from the dirty, gray clouds pressed in on me. Somewhere between one cold block and another, my breathing slowed. Guilt replaced my anger. It wasn't Gérald's mother's fault. Usually girls chose dresses, made gift lists, and enjoyed filling childhood hope chests with items they chose with their own mothers. I thought of my mom, alone at a kitchen table across the ocean on another continent, maybe daydreaming about her oldest daughter's wedding plans, maybe crying.

The next day, I received a letter from my Norwegian grandma:

> My dear eldest granddaughter,
>
> It is wonderful that you and Gérald, though born and raised worlds apart, should wed. That is fate. When I think of you, I am reminded of my own lovely wedding. Like you, I was 26 years old. I met your late Grandpa Gustav at a church picnic. When the phone company transferred him, we corresponded for three years. Then, he asked me to marry him. We had a delicious chicken dinner in the parlour of your great grandma Raymond's home on Lake Michigan. We took

the night train to Chicago to start our life together. Our marriage was short but happy. Twenty-three years later, Gustav died of cancer, leaving your mom, Russ, and Wayne to carry on the family name.

LOVE
Grandma Olson

Grandma always signed her letters with "love" printed in capitals so there was never any room for doubt. My tears smeared the black ink on the light blue stationery. Years later, history repeated itself. My mom left her mom on the east coast where Gram had relocated, to be with the man she loved in the Midwest. Mom put career plans on hold when babies popped out, one after the other. How did she cope with four kids underfoot, a husband who worked long hours to make ends meet, and a widowed mother living halfway across the United States? That was the way it was. But today's women have a choice. My mom was the first to remind me of the opportunities waiting.

Now what would Mom recommend? But Mom had long since stopped telling her spirited daughter what to do. I rocked on the bed, hugging my knees, thinking that in the old days life had been simpler. Women didn't have the chance to fly to Europe and fall in love with foreigners, to live with their boyfriends, or to test marriage.

I had no illusions. The honeymoon was over. I knew what it was like to bake bread three times a week, to wait in line for a half an hour for two pork chops at the butcher's, to be haunted by a smudged kitchen floor, dusty den, unmade bed. Ever the odd couple, Gérald even ate methodically, spreading butter to the corner of his bread. However, my shoes sprawled wherever they left my feet, my sweater lounged on the couch, my books lay open to the page where I left off. I thought his organization and my disarray would be the perfect balance.

But as the wedding approached, I burst into rage when Gérald suggested adding salt to the roast or dusting the den. Anger, like dirty laundry, piled up. One night, after missing my train, being caught in the rain and accosted by a stranger, I stomped into the apartment screaming.

"I hate Paris. People won't greet you like a human being,

but they'll grab at you like a piece of meat. I will give up my family and my country, but I refuse to live here."

"It won't be forever," Gérald said. "I'll find another job."

"You aren't looking for another job."

"We can't live without an income."

"Even if you found work in southern France, you'd never leave here, would you?" I challenged. "You want to stay in Paris to be close to your family?"

He leaped off the bed and strode into the kitchen and stared out the balcony window overlooking the cement courtyard enclosed by gray buildings. I tiptoed after him. I touched his slumped shoulder. When he turned his head, tears rolled down the hollows of his high cheekbones. I had never seen a him cry before. Now my fortress was crumbling, dissolving into salty human tears.

I eased my arm around him and pulled his head toward my chest and caressed his smooth, damp face. "Talk to me."

"I can't leave my family. I owe them everything. If we did move, where would we be? Really alone."

Reality was not a dream house in the country. It was this cramped apartment, these crowded streets. I did not say a word about my sacrifices. He read it in my eyes when I tore open airmail letters; he heard it in my voice when I answered long distance calls. But if this marriage were to work, I had to stop blaming him for the choices I had made.

After the fight, as if sedated, I lost myself in planning. When my younger sister, Karen, and my parents arrived the day before the wedding, I glowed as I served them a gourmet dinner in our mini kitchen. My dad's back leaned against the refrigerator; my mom almost sat in the sink, but the candlelight reflected contentment, not discomfort.

"For years, I tried to get her into the kitchen," my mom marveled, "but after a few months you have her cooking gourmet meals!"

"Pat used to boil brownies!" Karen teased.

When my dad boasted, "that was the best meal," I beamed. Then in the middle of dessert, my happiness melted as fast as the *mousse au chocolate*. I ran down the hall, flopped on the couch, and burst into tears.

Karen and Mom followed me and sat on one side of me, and Gérald sat on the other holding my hand. My dad stood by the window. "It's not fair to love two things with your whole heart and have to choose!"

"We want to hang onto you forever, but you belong to the world," Mom said. "Loving means letting go. One day you'll have a family of your own, then it won't be so hard."

She put her arm around me and rubbed my aching back. "I cried, too, the night before my wedding. I was only going to another state, not another country. You will always look back and wonder if you made the right decision. You'd wonder— even if you married an American."

Gérald patted my arm, offering silent reassurance. When I stopped crying, Karen kissed my cheek, Dad squeezed my hand and Mom touched my shoulder.

Later, long after Gérald fell asleep, I lay awake. My heart ached, as though someone I loved had just died. I mourned the part of myself that I was sacrificing. My weeping woke Gérald. He put his arm around me.

"You want to fly back to the States with your parents?" he asked, his voice cracking, "It's not too late."

We huddled together. For a long, long time, only the soft beating of our troubled hearts broke the silence of the black night. As dawn broke through our window, I squeezed Gérald's hand and whispered, "I don't want to leave you."

Then we rose, shared a cup of coffee and drove to Trouville for our wedding. I thought getting married anywhere but in the U.S.A. with all the fanfare would be easier. I was wrong. The ceremony started in the Hôtel de Ville, the mayor's office in Trouville. Our wedding was almost nullified because I couldn't find documentation proving my country was monogamous.

Our mayor in Courbevoie, where we lived, had to give permission for us to marry in another town. Since it was a double wedding, we listened to a monologue of names, dates and addresses, and signed a dozen official papers with eight different signatures, our witnesses and ours.

Then we drove five miles along the Normandy coast to a 17th century Catholic Church in Hennequeville. Red tape almost stopped us again. His sister wanted a church wedding. Gérald and I thought it would be simpler if we went along with what she wanted. It wasn't. I needed papers proving my baptism and, as a Protestant, required permission from the priest to marry in a Catholic church. Even Karen, as my witness, had to prove that she'd been baptized too. Gérald and

I were outraged.

Since we weren't getting married in the Trouville church in my husband's hometown, the priests also had to give permission for us to wed in Hennequeville. Then the bishop had to stamp his approval. The combination of demands by the Catholic Church and the French government would drive anyone of clear mind to elope.

In spite of the rigmarole, I beamed when I walked down the aisle in my electric blue dress, clinging to my proud father's arm to avoid toppling over in my electric blue high heels. Guests spilled out into the aisles of the tiny church. At the pulpit, I thanked the French for welcoming me into their country, then in German I thanked my German friends for celebrating with me, and lastly in English, I thanked my parents for teaching me how to love.

As the ceremony dragged on, Gérald and I clung to the chairs in front of us to keep from collapsing from back pain. No offense to God, but a Catholic wedding requires stamina.

The highlight of any French wedding is the reception dinner. Ours was held at Le Grand Bec restaurant on a cliff overlooking the sea. The seven-course meal was the most intricately planned part of the wedding. As I watched the bantering between my German friends, French in-laws, and American family, I grinned. For one glorious night, my three worlds came together, but it wasn't easy to orchestrate. My in-laws had been shocked when I announced, "The Germans are coming."

"Hubertus speaks English, so put him by Uncle Alain."

"But Alain can't speak English or German."

"That's okay. He has a good sense of humor."

"Put Bette between Claire and Pierre; she speaks French."

"Tom can sit by Frédérique. She knows some German."

"Don't worry," I told them, "after a few glasses of wine, we all speak the same language."

The real problem was how Gérald's grandparents, who survived the Occupation, would react. Papie, a member of the Gendarmerie Nationale during the war, once led the troops down the Champs Elysées liberating Paris.

At our wedding, he graciously welcomed guests by singing the American national anthem, German national anthem, and of course, the beloved Marseillaise.

After all our deliberation, places were changed, and courses were skipped. After appetizers, then pheasant pâté, and white fish in cream sauce, we aided digestion by imbibing in the famous *trou Normand,* sorbet with Calvados, a strong alcohol made from apples, a specialty from Normandy. Between courses, my sister Sue and brother Doug called from the States. They had graciously helped pay for Karen's flight to France. Then the meal resumed with roast beef, potatoes and beans, then salad. Alas, when the bell tolled, we had to forfeit the cheese course due to lack of time.

When the clock struck midnight, everyone circled the tables with kisses and Happy New Year's wishes for one another. Wedding guests donned party hats, tooted paper horns, and tossed colored streamers.

The French basketball club I was coaching and Gérald's volleyball team arrived, adding to the chaos. Champagne flowed. We pushed the tables aside. My Hubertus played the guitar, while my teammates from Marburg sang the tune of our old basketball lyric. We popped a cassette in the tape player and everyone, young and old, danced in couples or groups, or all alone. Even the priest swayed to the beat of American disco, German rock, and French love songs.

In the wee hours of the morning, a caravan of aunts, uncles and cousins followed us back to our honeymoon suite at our friends' Normand home. We spent our wedding night with dozens of relatives from Paris, Marseille, Rouen, and Sterling.

As the rest of the household slept, I lay awake thinking how perfect my imperfect wedding had been. By marrying into another culture, I would forgo the junk food, 24-hour TV, drive-in movie, carryout pizza, and Thanksgiving dinner. I would live with the inconvenience of laundry hanging about the apartment, clothes spilling out of cupboards, a refrigerator too small to stock. There would always be the daily shopping, the indifferent city, the longing for family. There would also be the man I loved. Some days that love may not be great enough to compensate for all my sacrifices. Maybe it wasn't just. But it had always been this way, for generations. I was a woman. I could bend and bridge the gap between worlds.

Our wedding celebration on New Year's Eve in 1983 united my German teammates, French relatives, and American family in a 17th century chapel in Normandy. By marrying the enemy, I chipped off a piece of barrier in the love/hate Franco-American relationship. From Norway to Normandy, the family bloodlines came full circle in our "Viking" marriage.

For months after my miscarriage, I imagined I was pregnant. Every time my period was a day late, I felt sick and hopeful. In March when my period was weeks overdue, and my belly hardened, I silently screamed in words scribbled across a blank white page

"Gérald, I think I'm pregnant," I told him that night.

"Your mind is tricking you," Gérald said without emotion.

"This time I am sure. It's a miracle!" I marveled. "What are the chances of getting pregnant while using birth control?"

Gérald continued eating dinner. When he didn't reply, I asked, "Aren't you happy?"

"I don't know; I don't want my life to change," he said. "But it's super!"

"I'm scared," I said. He reached across the table and squeezed my hand uniting us for an instant, until I broke the spell, "You'll be there with me during the delivery?"

"The delivery room? I don't really want to."

"Me either!" I shouted and pulled away from him. "I want a child, but you carry it. You get fat and ugly! You puke every morning! You give up your promotion to spoon baby food!"

As if slapped in the face, he looked stunned. Then, he stood up and walked out, closing the door, leaving me alone with bitterness. Why do women get all the jobs men don't want— like cooking, cleaning, and carrying babies? It would have been so much easier to eat, sleep, watch TV, and work 9 to 5. No, I had to feel new life cramping my abdomen and fear that my rage would destroy it again.

I pounded the bed with my fists until I was gasping. Then I opened an empty notebook. Anger spilled out on the page. "I don't want to feel sick and be so weary I could drop. I don't want to be strong enough for two. It still hurts every time I remember that icy table in a barren white room and silence, like a knife gouging my heart with guilt after I lost our baby."

When I heard the key in the lock, I leaped from the couch and threw my arms around Gérald.

"I am sorry," I said.

Gérald hugged me, and said, "You don't get it, do you?"

"Get what?"

"I love you because you are you."

"But I am unlovable. I am a bitch."

"That's an understatement! The problem is not my love, it's

yours."

"What!" I said. "I've been crazy about you since I first saw you. You're the best thing that ever happened to me."

"I don't doubt your feelings for me; the problem is you don't like yourself."

"I want to be healthy; I want to run. How can you stand me like this? A cripple."

"It would have been great to have a woman to share sports with," Gérald said taking my hand, "but I'll love you even if you can never ski down Mont Blanc with me. It's not perfect, but I'd rather have you like this than not at all."

"I can't make you happy. I can't cook. I hate cleaning. I'm not like French women."

"Maybe I like you because you are not French. So what if you hate the housework. You are a good listener. I admire your ability to embrace everyone."

I squeezed his hand and felt the courage to go on.

At my next obstetrician's checkup, the doctor calculated that February 10th was the date of conception. My attitude changed. Surely this diaphragm baby, conceived on the anniversary of my near-fatal car accident, was meant to be.

Though my emotional state improved, my physical state deteriorated. I felt like an old 45 album being played at 33 — dragging round and round. I walked around the apartment in T-shirts, admiring breasts that actually bounced, awed by my body's transformation, but burdened by the physical changes. As an athlete, I had controlled my body. Now nature ruled, rounding out my hips, belly, breasts, and thighs. The mirror, like a magnifying glass, transformed my body into a barrel. Physical discomfort reminded me of the miracle, but each new pain brought a new anxiety. Having a baby was a test of faith.

That autumn, I sat on the sidelines and watched the world waltz by, waiting for another passion to fill me with that same inner energy that basketball once did. I closed my eyes and felt my body going through all the motions, a jump shot, a behind the back dribble, a drive to the hoop. The loss would have never been so great had I never experienced the joy of movement. I was Pat, the athlete, not only in the public eye, but also in my own. I stared out the window, waiting and wondering if there would be life after basketball. And I prayed for a miracle, hoping that I could carry my baby safely into the world, knowing my heart would never withstand another loss.

I fought back from every set back. I got up; I moved on. However, I still reeled from the loss of my miscarriage.

Now even as I spun a new dream, I feared failure. Bringing any child into the world takes faith, but giving birth abroad demands fortitude. My second pregnancy was filled with anguish. After the summer in the States, my doctor's visit in Paris confirmed what I had feared — something was wrong.

"The pains you have are contractions. The baby dropped too early and its head is pushing against your cervix. You must stay in bed to prevent a premature delivery."

That night I fell into a fitful sleep and dreamed I gave birth to an electronic baby that disintegrated when I changed his diapers. I woke up, screaming, when a sharp pain stabbed my pelvis. "Aïe," I cried grasping my abdomen.

"Are you okay?" Gérald asked, looking alarmed.

"I'm fine," I said, squeezing his hand. "Let's pick a name."

Our child's language dilemmas began with choosing a first name that could be pronounced coherently in English and in French. We scribbled our top five favorites of either gender on scraps of paper and tossed them into a Chicago Bulls' cap. At 2 a.m., awake from jet lag and anxiety, we drew our firstborn's given name out of a hat.

The next day, I felt compelled to call my deeply religious teammate to tell her about my new pregnancy and old fears.

"When are you due?" Vonnie asked.

"In November," I said.

"March, April, May ..." I listened as Vonnie counted the months aloud. "Pat, you got pregnant a year after the day you should have died in the accident! This baby is a miracle!"

When I moved abroad, I absorbed the French way of life wholeheartedly. In the ultimate makeover, my hair chopped into a pixie, my eyes painted in black mascara, I adopted the aura of femme fatale. In fashionable restaurants in the Latin Quarter, I sampled cow tongue and slurped raw oysters, feigning an exquisite French palate for delicacies, including those that gagged me. But in my seventh month of pregnancy, too nauseated to stomach buttered toast, French cuisine was out of the question. Each day that I still carried the baby, I gave a silent prayer. A week later, I returned to the doctor's office for a check up since my cervix dilated too early.

"Tsk, tsk, Madame! You no stand, no sit, no walk," the doctor said. "Or zee bébé come tomorrow."

"Can I swim?"

"Shvim?" He looked bewildered. "No one ask dis. Maybe okay. You off zee feet."

So every other day, Junior and I ventured out into the real world and swam laps, and shared that warm, free, floating feeling, like in the womb.

If I disobeyed doctor's orders and walked ten yards to the bakery, my stomach knotted up into a tight ball. I imagined the little, old lady behind me saying," *Excusez-moi, Madame,* I think you dropped something."

Oops! There goes Junior.

As if drugged, I dragged myself from the couch to the bed. My lower back ached. Every time I stood up my uterus contracted as if my body had a built-in warning system, so I lay back down feeling destined to remain a fat, pregnant invalid forever.

At my next visit, the doctor assured me I had made it past the danger point. "If you haven't started labor by November 1, we'll induce it so you won't get unnecessary stretch marks."

I giggled. Only in France. They delivered babies ten days early for aesthetic appeal. For convenience, my doctor set a time and date to induce labor.

Each day after I reached my full-term date, I walked faster and farther, hoping to speed up the process. Then I'd stop to rest on the same park bench I sat on four years ago when I first moved abroad. Back then, I listened to the Parisian children babble, their words like music I'd never heard before. Without language comprehension, I saw the world anew through the eyes of a child. Everything, from unlocking a door to buying bread, had had to be relearned.

Seasons, like the red, orange and brown leaves, kept turning. Chestnuts dropped to the damp earth and the golden sun winked through the Parisian clouds. The language of children was no longer foreign, for I grew up all over again in another country. Now I was a woman bearing a child to carry on the new dreams where mine left off.

"You're still here!" said the butcher pointing at my protruding belly. "Tonight will be the night. It's a full moon."

The night before labor was induced, we celebrated with a meal out. At least Gérald celebrated. I picked at my steak and glared at him, annoyed at his ravenous appetite and childish enthusiasm. How could he act happy when he knew tomorrow

I would suffer? While Gérald slept, in a change of emotion so common among pregnant women, I wrote him a note.

"After my accident, I prayed for the strength to carry our baby. Raising our child between worlds will never be easy, but he or she will always be easy to love — a reflection of the daddy I adore."

In the morning, I raged in anger. While Gérald rushed to pack my bag, I dressed in slow motion. My hands shook as I tied my shoes. My body already missed the pattern of rolling, kicking, and moving that was so much a part of me. At the hospital, the nurse injected an IV in my arm with glucose and a hormone to induce labor. Gérald coached me through the contractions. "Take a deep breath. Inhale. Exhale. Relax."

In the beginning, the delivery was like a game. Then my hands and feet went numb. I vomited bile. The contractions controlled my body. I panicked. "I don't want this baby; I want the pain to be over." For an instant I stared into Gérald's eyes and hated him for his masculinity, his inability to share this agony. My breathing was erratic; my legs shook. I dug my nails into Gérald's arm and yelled at the doctor, "I have to push."

"Get the anesthesiologist," he said. "Forget it. No time left."

Minutes later, while the doctor stitched me, my weightless body floated between the floor and the ceiling. Gérald beamed. As soon as our baby gave us the big bonjour at 1:20 p.m., the doctor and nurses, in typical French fashion, left for lunch.

"Isn't she the most beautiful baby?" I cooed, touching her squished nose and counting her fingers and toes. Later in our hospital room, a tiny heart fluttered against my own. I lay her across my stomach and felt her arms and legs kick on the outside, instead of inside, while the sun shone through the windows blessing our miracle baby.

Within the span of one horrific year, I had lost everything — my athleticism, my career, my pregnancy — yet I never quit. The end of one life signals the beginning of another. I conceived a new dream and named her Nathalie. On October 27, 1984, as God winked in the sunlight blinking through the clouds, I cradled my newborn to my breast and entered a whole new ballgame.

Four thousand miles away in Chicago my sister Sue dreamed, "It's a girl!" My dad replaced his baseball cap with a French beret and handed out bubble gum cigars to Phil and his colleagues at Sterling High. And in Eureka my proud grandpa, Coach Mac, received another congratulatory letter from one of his "boys" living at the White House. This baby, with eyes the color of the skies where fjords met the heavens in Norway, was destined to unite people.

Epilogue

On November 29, 2004, long after my career as an athlete ended, I received a letter inducting Pat McKinzie, "former Sterling High School stand out and Illinois State All- American player" into the Illinois Basketball Coaches Hall of Fame. I reread the letter twice thinking, "Who's that girl?" Thirty some years ago that girl moved abroad to pursue her goal to play basketball professionally until an accident shattered that dream and left that girl—me—sidelined permanently.

The image of a lean, long-limbed girl flicking a ponytail as I drove the baseline in a red, pinstriped uniform fades in my memory. But I can still feel the ball leaving my fingertips, arching upwards in hope toward that orange circle in the sky.

Today, I drive the school bus to games, tape injuries, and set the score table before I even begin the chalk talk passing down stories that shaped me. I learned from the best. My father Jim McKinzie, my mentor Phil Smith, and my college coach Jill Hutchison. All three pioneers promoted gender equity. Henry Fields became my tutor in international ball, but our friendship would never have developed without my family's upbringing teaching tolerance.

But the coach who had the greatest impact on my life was my grandpa. Although inspired by the legendary Coach Ralph "Mac" McKinzie, I had no aspirations of coaching a future President. Yet, who can say? I never dreamed I would one day be teaching sons and daughters of diplomats, ambassadors, and world leaders. One never knows how much the right word, at the right time, can shape an athlete.

If it takes a village to raise a child, it takes a team to make an athlete, male or female. Teams force the individual player to check his or her ego at the door. Teams demand commitment. Teams give players the courage to go on when they feel like giving up.

Years ago, a player on my least talented team in Paris wrote me a letter. "After a long battle with cystic fibrosis, my twin brother died in my arms. I wanted to die too, but I never gave up. You taught me to keep fighting."

When I played basketball, nobody knew my name. No matter. The only glory I needed was the joy in running down the court. Never mind that I fell short of my greatest dream: my professional team folded, my French team banned foreigners in my first year, and my season in Germany ended in a car accident. But, I stayed in the game.

The day the athlete in me died, a coach was born, reluctantly. At the end of every season, I swear I will retire; but every fall I return to the gym. Indebted to the coaches who believed in me at a time when no one believed in girls, today I instill fundamentals from the Heartland — discipline, tolerance, and integrity — into athletes from around the world.

How do I know what to say in those pre-game chalk talks, half-time pep rallies, and last minute timeouts? I don't. Words, like sermons of divine intervention plucked out of air from voices of my past (Grandpa, Dad, Phil, Jill, and Henry) speak through me to the next generation of athletes. My underlying theme, the same each season, builds the foundation of teamwork by instilling respect for others. Naismith founded a team game that he claimed, "is easy to play, but hard to master," to bring people of all nationalities and walks of life together. My gift is the game itself. In an age of alienation, when it is easier to hook up in cyberspace than to communicate between different races, religions, nations, genders and generations, teams break down the barriers. Teams force us to connect "woman to woman." Teams give us a sense of belonging. The round ball mimics our globe. What "goes round comes round in life and love and basketball." Coaches, players, fans, and referees are part of that ideal team, that perfect dream — that somehow through our love of the game we can create a better world.

My home is in Europe, but my roots remain in the Midwest. In 1984, though I was not present for my Induction to the Illinois State University Hall of Fame, my lifelong coach, Dad, attended to receive my honor and, fittingly, my college coach, Jill Hutchison, was there being inducted too. An ocean away, I toasted that ghost of a girl who grew up, not so long ago, dreaming of playing ball like the boys, a dream nurtured on the playing fields of Illinois, a dream that the passage of Title IX made possible. That gal may be long gone, but her spirit lives on in every girl who grows up shooting skyward toward her own hoop dreams.

When I lament that I cannot ski the Alps, run marathons, or travel the world because injury forced early "retirement" from playing basketball, I focus on what I can do. I can write letters, give pep talks, encourage students, and offer support to family and friends. As I write this, I am flat on my back, typing on a laptop while resting the spine. This is not the life I envisioned. Oh no, I was going to conquer the world straight up.

I spent the first half of my life fighting to be allowed on the playing fields and the second half on the sideline learning how to graciously cheer for others to reach their goals. As a McKinzie, I set high standards and then berated myself when I fell short. Because I never made it to the pinnacle of my dreams to become an Olympian, I felt my life was a failure. Then, I set an equally lofty goal, to write a book. After dozens of drafts and representation by three agents over three decades, I put the manuscript away and mourned the loss.

"I am so sick of hearing about that damn book," Gérald, the CEO of a Swiss printing company said to me. "The publishing world is upended. Your life has been about never giving up—why don't you publish it yourself?"

Herein lies a lifetime of stops and starts, drafts and redrafts, tears and fears. And hope. It epitomizes my own I'll-do-it-myself lifestyle that I adopted as a feisty child.

Only after observing myself through the eyes of Tara, a former student/athlete, who edited my book, could I see the light.

"It's not about the despair or anger or frustration that each challenge threw at you, but it is about the way you handle each hurdle, the way you get up and fight and ask for more, and the way your family and friends and you interact – and finally, the way that your almost perfect life just comes out of nowhere. You became a successful woman living in a foreign country with a career and family, having lived on next to nothing except your dreams," Tara said.

"THAT Pat, THAT is what you should be sharing with the readers in the end. You have achieved more than you ever dreamed of shaping young women, teaching not just basketball skills but life skills and team skills and about dreams and how you always need to strive for them. Your book shows the readers that not having dreams or letting them go because they think they can't achieve them THAT is the failure. And with Title IX comes extra responsibilities and

Made in the USA
Lexington, KY
10 August 2013